CYBER SAFE

i

CYBER SAFE

Protecting Yourself and Your Family in the Digital Age

DAVID W. EVANS

DUKE SPRUCE
ENTERPRISES

CYBER
SAFE

DUKE SPRUCE
ENTERPRISES

Illustrated and Written by David W. Evans

ISBN: 979-8-9993883-1-5 (Hardcopy), ISBN: 979-8-9993883-0-8 (Paperback),
ISBN: 979-8-9993883-2-2 (eBook)

Dedication

Authoring this book has been an incredible journey, made possible by the love, support, guidance, and encouragement of so many people.

Most importantly, to my family, primarily, to my wife, Mikealene. Your unwavering support and belief in me, patience through long nights of technological work, and constant encouragement kept me going throughout my career and my life. Your impact on my life has been immeasurable. And to my sons, Jacob, Joshua, and Jaden, thank you for filling my days with joy, the rewarding experience of fatherhood, and reminding me why persistence matters. Also, to my parents, Charles, and Violet, for your guidance, love, wisdom, and lifelong belief in my potential have shaped me into who I am today. Your influence is present on every page of this book.

To my wife, children, and parents, I dedicate this book.

You lock your doors at night. It is time to do the same online.

In a world built from code, security is the foundation. Without it, the structures we trust collapse into chaos.

"Security is not a product, but a process."
— *Bruce Schneier*

Table of Contents

Foreward

The risk of cyberattacks, stealing our most sensitive data for ransom or public exposure, is a pervasive threat both in the United States and globally. Even highly sophisticated technology corporations and one of the best developers of cybersecurity protection systems like Cisco have found themselves vulnerable. In May 2022, for instance, Cisco discovered a breach involving voice phishing attacks that targeted an employee's Google account. The aftermath saw the ransomware gang Yanluowang posting leaked files online, a stark reminder of how persistent and inventive attackers have become.

The escalating threat has prompted action at the highest levels. The U.S. Federal Bureau of Investigation leads the National Cyber Investigative Joint Task Force, a coalition of over thirty agencies established in 2008 to combat cyber threats. Meanwhile, businesses and individuals increasingly turn to cybersecurity insurance as part of their defense strategies. Yet, despite these efforts, cyberattacks persist, driven by ever-evolving schemes to penetrate our defenses.

In this context, the role of a technology executive extends far beyond managing systems, it is about safeguarding the very fabric of modern life. Technology is not just a tool; It is a transformative force reshaping industries, communities, and lives. This book captures the experience of one such leader, David Evans, a visionary who not only implemented innovative cybersecurity measures for decades but also fostered connectivity and resilience in one of the world's most technologically advanced cities.

As Chief Information Officer for Kansas City, Missouri, a municipality of over 500,000 residents within a metro area of more than two million, David has worked on the front lines of technology and cybersecurity. His collaborations with the Department of Homeland Security, state, local and federal law enforcement exemplify a holistic approach to protecting his city from cyber threats. His efforts extend beyond technology, reflecting a profound understanding of the intersection between resilience, innovation, and human responsibility.

David's expertise has made him a sought-after national speaker. I was privileged to witness his insights firsthand at a CHUBB cyber insurance conference that I helped organize. At this event, hosted by my law firm, Resnick and Louis, P.C., and CHUBB Insurance, David spoke eloquently on the interplay between cybersecurity and cyber insurance. His presentation stood out not for its theoretical content, but for its practical, real-world solutions informed by years of firsthand experience. His message was clear: user resilience depends on a deep understanding of the risks and responsibilities inherent in the digital age.

This book distills David's remarkable journey and expertise into a practical guide for navigating the complexities of our interconnected world. It offers a roadmap not just for cybersecurity professionals but for anyone striving to safeguard themselves or their organizations in an era defined by rapid technological advancement. Beyond professional development, this book is a blueprint for fostering innovation, resilience, and informed decision-making.

The time-honored adage, "Forewarned is forearmed," has never been more relevant. David Evans' insights will equip readers with the tools to understand, adapt to, and overcome the challenges of cybersecurity, providing a foundation for a sustainable, tech-driven future. I am honored to introduce this invaluable resource; written by a leader whose vision and expertise continue to shape a safer digital world.

Roger W. Strassburg
Partner, Resnick and Louis, P.C.
National Cybersecurity Advocate and Legal Expert

Preface

Over the years, I have delivered presentations and performed speaking engagements on cybersecurity to a diverse array of audiences. These have ranged from new employee orientations, city council meetings to national radio broadcasts and major conferences. The audiences have included individuals concerned about personal technology risks, as well as large organizations and governments focused on preventing catastrophic cyberattacks.

One common request I have encountered during these engagements has been for accessible cybersecurity education, resources that cater to personal learning to large-scale organizational preparedness.

This book is designed to provide essential cybersecurity knowledge to empower individuals. My goal is to present material that is both easily understandable for everyday users and advanced defense methods sufficiently detailed for those willing to deepen their skills. By building and strengthening cybersecurity awareness and expertise at all levels, we can collectively reduce risks and create a safer digital environment for everyone.

Understanding Content Levels in This Book

This book includes both basic and advanced cybersecurity topics, clearly marked to guide your learning. Two symbols help identify the importance and complexity of each section:

- 🔑 **Core Essentials** – These are must-know practices that every home user should understand and apply to stay protected online. They form the foundation of safe digital habits and align with CISA's top ten recommendations for home users.
- 🛡 **Advanced Protection** – These topics offer stronger security but may require some advanced technical skill or understanding.

Each chapter is labeled with a symbol to indicate its overall content level for that chapter. However, you may see a symbol applied to a specific topic indicating that topic's specific content level. If you are comfortable exploring deeper topics, feel free to dive in. If something seems too advanced, do not worry, just skip ahead. If you are grasping the 🔑 key concepts, you will still have the essential tools needed for a strong basic defense. Every security improvement you make, big or small, helps reduce your exposure to cyber risks.

Introduction

Welcome to the digital age, where everything from our bank accounts and private messages to health records and family photos lives online. Every day, new advancements bring more of our personal information into the world of technology. We enjoy incredible convenience and access to limitless information, but this interconnected world also comes with risks that many are not fully prepared to manage.

Cybersecurity is no longer just a concern for large corporations or governments; it affects everyone, including you. One of the topics I often address when speaking at public events is the growing number of technological products people rely on, many of which they do not even realize they are using daily. Information Technology is not just computers now and has not been for decades. Most individuals are unaware of how many systems they interact with or how quickly changes in our lives or culture can accelerate the adoption of innovative technologies.

A striking example is the recent pandemic. In response to COVID-19, society rapidly shifted to a work-from-home culture to maintain continuity while assessing the scope of the crisis. We also saw widespread adoption of touchless technologies, such as contactless payments, digital health apps, facial recognition, and remote check-ins, to reduce cross-contamination. While these innovations enhanced hygiene and convenience, they also introduced serious cybersecurity vulnerabilities. The fast rollout of mobile apps and cloud-based services expanded attack surfaces, often without thorough security evaluations. Personal health data, biometric identifiers, and payment credentials became prime targets for cybercriminals, raising urgent concerns about data privacy, system integrity, and the resilience of digital solutions. This is also not the end of technological advancement. The adoption of innovative technologies will continue to accelerate for the foreseeable future. It is time to accept the reality: you, too, are a target.

This book is your practical, easy-to-understand guide to protecting yourself in an increasingly digital world. Cybercrime is no longer confined to obscure hackers targeting corporations, it now includes professional cybercriminals, terrorist organizations, and state-sponsored warfare. These threats appear as phishing emails in your inbox, fraudulent text messages on your phone, and malware embedded in seemingly harmless apps. Whether you use the internet for banking, social media, shopping, or entertainment, understanding how to protect your information is essential or it could cost you dearly someday.

But do not worry, Cybersecurity does not have to be complicated. This book breaks down intimidating topics like passwords, privacy settings, phishing scams, and safe browsing into straightforward, actionable advice. You do not need to be a tech expert to protect yourself; all you need is a bit of knowledge and a few good habits. The goal of this book is to provide clear, practical information to help you better protect yourself, as well as more in-depth content if you wish to dive deeper.

Here is what you will learn:
- Protect your personal information from identity theft and fraud.
- Create strong, memorable passwords (and finally stop using "password123").
- Recognize phishing attempts to avoid scams from fake websites and emails.
- Secure your devices. From your phone to smart home gadgets, against malware and unauthorized access.
- Adjust social media privacy settings to keep your personal life private.
- Develop cybersecurity habits that will serve you well.

You do not need to become a cybersecurity expert to stay safe online, but knowing the basics can make all the difference. This book will empower you to take control of your digital life with confidence, so you can enjoy the benefits of technology without constantly worrying about threats.

Remember: Cybersecurity is a shared responsibility. Each of us plays a role in building a safer internet, every vulnerable user adds risk to everyone else. With the right mindset and knowledge, you can do your part and rest easier knowing your information is safer.

While this book does not cover the cybersecurity details of every application or the full breadth of today's complex technology landscape, it provides essential knowledge and practical steps that will significantly elevate your security posture. The strategies and tools shared here are designed to help you take immediate action, guiding you from uncertainty to confidence. You may not become an expert overnight, but by the time you finish this book, you will be far more secure than you were when you started.

So, let us dive in and explore how you can become your own first line of defense. It is time to take control of your digital world, because in today's connected life, you are responsible for the safety of your technologies and data, and you are your best defense.

PROTECTING YOUR ASSETS AND YOU

Chapter 1

Understanding the Basics of Cybersecurity

With our growing reliance on technology, threats and data breaches are becoming increasingly common. So, it is extremely important for individuals to understand the scope of technologies they are using that could be at risk. In today's digital world, personal computers are just one piece of a much broader technology landscape. From smartphones and smart TVs to home assistants, wearable devices, and connected appliances, individuals are surrounded by technology that constantly communicates over the internet. Each of these devices increases convenience but also expands the potential attack surface for cyber threats. As the breadth of technology grows, so does the importance of understanding and addressing the cybersecurity vulnerabilities that come with it. While companies often have dedicated IT teams to manage cyber threats, home users are left vulnerable. These advances in technology are innovative, intriguing, and convenient, however they also pose a new set of security risks.

Cybercriminals frequently target individuals because personal systems often lack sophisticated defenses. Simple attacks, such as tricking users into clicking on dangerous links, can lead to devastating consequences like identity theft or bank fraud. According to the FBI's Cybersecurity and Infrastructure Security Agency (CISA), more than 90% of successful cyber-attacks now start with these types of attacks. That means, the individual operating the device is inviting the attacker in and usually with full access. This book is a great start in gaining knowledge and confidence to protect your digital home.

Why Would I or my Home be a Target?

You and your home can be a target for cyberattacks due to a variety of factors:

- **Valuable Personal Data:** Attackers seek financial info, personal details, and online account credentials, which can be used for identity theft or sold on the dark web.
- **Weak Security:** Many home users leave default passwords on devices, fail to update software, or lack knowledge of cybersecurity best practices.
- **Unsecured Smart Devices:** Connected devices like smart TVs, cameras, and voice assistants are often overlooked and lack strong security, making them easy targets.
- **Home Networks:** Home internet equipment and weak Wi-Fi passwords or outdated encryption can expose your entire network,

allowing attackers to access all the devices you own.

- **Financial Gains:** Cybercriminals use ransomware to extort money, or hijack systems in your home to perform "cryptomining" (using your systems and electricity to generate cryptocurrency for them) and in the end, drastically elevating your electricity bills. Electricity is the most expensive component of generating cryptocurrency.
- **Remote Work Vulnerabilities:** Home offices are now prime targets as attackers attempt to breach corporate networks through unsecured home systems. *I witnessed an instance where a corporate user account was used to perform cybercrime, and the FBI commandeered the employees' home technology systems to perform forensics.*
- **Phishing & Scams:** Home users are frequently targeted by phishing emails, phone scams, and social engineering attacks.
- **Low Detection Rates:** Homes and home users typically lack sophisticated security systems and skills, making it easier for attackers to operate undetected.
- **Cryptocurrency Theft:** The anonymity of cryptocurrencies makes them an ideal target for hackers. Stolen funds are laundered and used to support terrorist organizations like ISIS and al-Qaeda.
- **State-Sponsored Cybercrime:** Cybersecurity attacks are increasingly used to fund warfare and other kinds of conflicts:
  o Some governments, such as Russia, support cybercriminal groups like Evil Corp to steal millions of dollars, potentially funding military operations.
  o State-sponsored hackers, like those from North Korea, conduct large-scale cyber heists (e.g., the $81 million Bangladesh Bank robbery) to finance missile and nuclear programs.
- **Global Security Impact:** These attacks not only fund conflict but also destabilize economies, erode trust in digital systems, and contribute to political instability.
- In essence, cyberattacks have become a modern method of generating revenue for warfare, supporting both state and non-state actors in their military activities.
- In short, homes are increasingly targeted because they often have weaker security measures, contain valuable data, and can serve as practice grounds or gateways for larger attacks. A simple successful attack of a

single person can spread to millions of systems and become a major disaster. Hence the title virus. Securing your network, updating devices, and using strong passwords can help protect against these risks and costs for countless others.

Identity Theft and Data Breaches

Identity theft occurs when attackers gain access to your personal information, like your social security number, address, or bank account details, and use it to:

- Open new lines of credit in your name.
- Apply for loans, credit cards, or mortgages.
- File fraudulent tax returns for refunds or claim benefits.
- Essentially, anything you can do with your personal information, so can they.

Even seemingly small leaks of personal data can have grave consequences. For example, a **data breach at a healthcare provider** could expose your name, address, relatives' names, medical history, insurance details, or social security number, putting you at risk of fraud.

Many identity theft victims are not immediately aware of the theft. It can take months or even years to discover that a criminal has been using your identity. Here is a quick look at the odds you will be compromised at some point:

- Odds of winning the Powerball lottery, 1 in 292,201,338, but some people will sink tons of money on this gamble.
- Odds of your house burning, 1 in 3,000, but people acquire home insurance.
- Odds of your identity getting stolen in your lifetime are 1 in 4, but most people are unaware of the threat or will ignore it entirely.

The CIA Triad: Confidentiality, Integrity, Availability

The CIA Triad forms the foundation of cybersecurity:

- **Confidentiality:** Protect data from unauthorized access.
- **Integrity:** Ensure information is accurate and not tampered with.
- **Availability:** Keep systems accessible when needed.

The Importance of Personal Cybersecurity

Personal cybersecurity is not just about protecting devices; it is about safeguarding your personal identity, financial information and assets, and peace of mind. Even minor breaches, such as hacked social media accounts, can result in lasting consequences, including reputational damage or monetary loss. Cybersecurity efforts also extend to protecting family members, especially children and elderly individuals who may not fully understand online dangers.

Case Studies: Real-World Examples of Home Cybersecurity Breaches

Case 1: One notable case of a home user experiencing a cybersecurity breach involved a person named Amy in New York, who fell victim to a sophisticated phishing scam in 2020. Amy received an email that appeared to be from her bank, claiming that there had been "suspicious activity" on her account. The email looked authentic, with bank logos and realistic formatting, and it urged her to click a link to verify her account information.

Feeling alarmed, Amy clicked on the link, which led to a webpage almost identical to her bank's official site. She entered her login credentials and other personal details as prompted. Unbeknownst to her, this information went directly to the hackers, who quickly used it to gain access to her bank account. Over the next few days, they withdrew thousands of dollars in multiple transactions, leaving Amy's account nearly empty.

By the time Amy realized something was wrong, the hackers had already transferred the funds through a series of untraceable accounts. She reported the incident to her bank and law enforcement, but recovering the lost money proved difficult and time-consuming, given the sophisticated methods used to disguise the transactions. Ultimately, Amy only recovered a portion of the stolen funds, while the rest was unrecoverable.

This incident underscores the financial risks that home users face if they fall victim to phishing attacks and other cybersecurity threats. It also highlights the importance of verifying suspicious emails directly with institutions, enabling multi-factor authentication, and staying vigilant to avoid costly breaches like Amy's.

Case 2: A high-profile case of a home user experiencing a ransomware attack involved a man named Steve in California in 2019. Steve, an avid photographer, used his personal computer to store thousands of family photos, personal documents, and business files. One day, while browsing the web, he unknowingly downloaded a file containing a ransomware virus, called "Ryuk."

As soon as the ransomware was installed, it began encrypting all the files on his computer, rendering them inaccessible. A message appeared on his screen, demanding a ransom payment in Bitcoin in exchange for a decryption key to unlock his files. The message warned that if he did not pay within 72 hours, the ransom amount would double, and after a week, the key would be permanently destroyed, making his data unrecoverable.

Steve, desperate to recover years of irreplaceable memories and essential business files, reached out to cybersecurity experts for advice. They recommended paying the ransom, as there was no guarantee the attackers would honor the agreement. However, he had no recent backups, so Steve eventually decided to pay the ransom, costing him over $1,000 in Bitcoin.

After paying, Steve received the decryption key, but only about half of his files were recoverable, and some were permanently corrupted. The ransomware attack left him with both emotional distress and monetary loss, and he was motivated to improve his cybersecurity practices, such as regularly backing up his data, using antivirus software, and being cautious about suspicious downloads.

This case emphasizes the importance of regular backups, updated antivirus software, and caution when downloading files or clicking links online, as ransomware can cause severe personal and financial harm to home users.

Case 3: A widely reported case of a home user experiencing a cybersecurity breach involved a Texas couple whose baby monitor was hacked. The couple had installed a Wi-Fi-connected baby monitor in their infant's room to keep an eye on their child while they were in other areas of the house. However, one night, they heard strange voices coming from their child's room. When they investigated, they discovered that someone had hacked into the baby monitor and was remotely controlling it, even speaking to their child.

The hacker had accessed the device through the home's Wi-Fi network, exploiting weak security on the baby monitor and gaining control over its camera and microphone. This incident highlighted the vulnerabilities of smart home devices, particularly when default passwords are used or when devices lack strong encryption. The breach was highly unsettling for the family, as it intruded on their private space and exposed their young child to the actions of a stranger.

Following this incident, the couple replaced the monitor with a more secure model and increased their home network's security settings. The case underscored the importance of securing internet-connected devices, changing default passwords, and being mindful of privacy risks associated with IoT (Internet of Things) devices in the home.

The Potential Impact of a Cybersecurity Breach

Cybersecurity breaches have inflicted substantial financial losses worldwide. They can begin on a single device and replicate to millions of devices in a brief period. Preventing the first attack is the key. Below is an overview of the costliest cyberattacks to date:

1. **NotPetya Attack (2016):** NotPetya or Petya is the name of the malware discovered in 2016. It is inspired by a fictional Soviet satellite from the James Bond movie GoldenEye (1995). Once activated, it would gain

administrative access, overwrite the Master Boot Record (MBR) to encrypt your hard drive. Files on an infected computer were not lost or corrupted; they were simply inaccessible unless the victim paid a ransom in bitcoins only to decrypt their information. The White House estimated the total damage of these attacks to exceed $10 billion, making it one of the most destructive cyberattacks ever. Following is a sample screenshot of an attacked system.

Sample NotPetya Attack Screen

```
Ooops. your important files are encrypted.

If you see this text  then your files are no longer accessible, because they
have been encrypted.  Perhaps you are busy looking for a way to recover your
files, but don't waste your time.  Nobody can recover your files without our
decryption service

We guarantee that you can recover all your files safely and easily.  All you
need to do is submit the payment and purchase the decryption key.

Please follow the instructions:

1  Send $300 worth of Bitcoin to following address:

   1Mz7153HMuxXTuR2R1t78wGSdzaAtNbBWX

2  Send your Bitcoin wallet ID and personal installation key to e-mail
   wowsmith123456@posteo.net. Your personal installation key:

   zRNagE-CDBMfc-pD5Ai4-vFd5d2-14whs5-d7UCzb-RYJq3E-ANg8rX-49XFX2-Ed2R5A

If you already purchased your key, please enter it below.
Key: _
```

2. **MyDoom Worm (2004)**: First discovered in late January 2004, the MyDoom worm quickly earned a notorious reputation among cybersecurity professionals. Designed to exploit vulnerabilities in Microsoft Windows systems, this malicious software launched an unprecedented global infection campaign via email. At its peak, MyDoom became the fastest-spreading worm in internet history, outpacing infamous predecessors like SoBig and ILOVEYOU, a record that still stands as of 2025.

Initially dismissed by many users as simple junk mail, the worm's true impact revealed itself over time. Estimates suggest that over half a million systems were compromised during its primary wave of attacks. The financial toll was staggering, with losses calculated at roughly $38 billion at the time, a figure that adjusts to more than $52 billion in today's economy.

At the height of its activity, MyDoom was estimated to be responsible for as much as a quarter of all global email traffic. Remarkably, despite the passage of decades, traces of MyDoom persist in modern internet traffic. It is believed to account for about 1% of all phishing attempts today. Given that approximately 3.4 billion phishing emails are sent daily, that puts MyDoom's continued output at over a billion messages per year, a striking legacy for a worm born two decades ago.

3. **SoBig Virus (2003)**: In August 2003, the SoBig worm unleashed a widespread digital assault, infecting millions of Microsoft Windows-based systems around the globe. Propagating rapidly through email, SoBig caused major operational setbacks across organizations, resulting in an estimated $37.1 billion in global economic damage. This figure encompasses losses across North America, Europe, and Asia.

   Though traces of early development were reportedly observed as far back as August 2002, the first version, identified as SoBig.A, surfaced publicly in January 2003. What followed was a series of increasingly aggressive variants: SoBig.B appeared on May 18, initially referred to as "Palyh" before researchers confirmed its lineage as part of the SoBig family. This continued through many variants. The most damaging iteration, SoBig.F, debuted on August 19, 2003. This version overwhelmed email systems with such volume that it set records for email-based malware traffic at the time. Its ability to self-replicate and send mass emails made it one of the most pervasive worms in internet history.

   As of 2018, SoBig remains ranked as the second-fastest spreading computer worm ever recorded, trailing only behind MyDoom in terms of sheer reach and impact.

4. **Sasser and Netsky Worms (2004) - Teen-Created Worms with Global Consequences:** A pair of highly disruptive computer worms, Sasser, and Netsky, were traced back to Sven Jaschan, a 17-year-old German computer science student at the time of their creation. Exploiting known vulnerabilities in Microsoft Windows systems, these worms caused significant global disruptions across sectors ranging from media to aviation.

In 2004, shortly after turning 18, Jaschan was apprehended by authorities following a $250,000 reward offered for information leading to the creator of the Sasser worm. His arrest came after a tip from an acquaintance, who revealed that Jaschan was responsible for both the Sasser worm and a particularly damaging strain of the Netsky virus, known as Netsky.AC. Collectively, the financial toll of these attacks was estimated at around $31 billion.

Sasser's spread was especially impactful, disabling systems in major organizations. Notably, the French news agency Agence France-Presse (AFP) experienced hours-long satellite communication outages, while Delta Air Lines was forced to cancel several international flights due to operational failures.

Despite its rapid spread, Sasser could be neutralized with the proper security measures in place. Systems protected by firewalls or kept up to date with Microsoft's available patches were generally safe from infection. In fact, the specific vulnerability exploited by Sasser had been identified and patched prior to the worm's release, highlighting the importance of timely software updates.

Meanwhile, Netsky variants, also authored by Jaschan, circulated widely during the same period. One notable feature of Netsky infections was the appearance of a shutdown timer, which alerted users that their systems were being forced to reboot, an alarming signal of compromise. Together, Sasser and Netsky demonstrated how a single individual with technical knowledge and malicious intent could disrupt millions of machines worldwide, underscoring the critical need for proactive cybersecurity.

5. **WannaCry Ransomware (2017):** In May 2017, a devastating ransomware outbreak known as WannaCry stunned organizations

around the world. Within days, the malware had infected more than 200,000 systems across over 150 countries. The primary targets were computers running outdated or unpatched versions of Microsoft Windows. Once infected, affected machines had their files encrypted, with the attacker's demanding payment in Bitcoin to unlock the data.

The worm-like spread of WannaCry was made possible by a Windows vulnerability known as EternalBlue, a cyber-weapon originally developed by the U.S. National Security Agency (NSA). This exploit was made public just a month earlier, when a hacking group calling itself The Shadow Brokers leaked several NSA tools online. Although Microsoft had issued a security update addressing the EternalBlue vulnerability two months before the attack, many systems remained exposed due to delayed patching or reliance on unsupported operating systems.

WannaCry's global disruption was eventually brought to a halt when a 22-year-old British cybersecurity researcher accidentally discovered a built-in kill switch, a specific domain name the malware queried before executing. Registering that domain effectively neutralized further spread. The economic impact of WannaCry was enormous, with estimated losses exceeding $4 billion due to business interruptions, recovery costs, and ransom demands. The attack affected critical services, including healthcare systems, transportation networks, and corporate IT infrastructures.

WannaCry became a stark reminder of how crucial it is to maintain up-to-date security practices. Regular software updates, timely patching, and strong backup strategies remain among the most effective defenses against ransomware and similar threats. Here is a sample screenshot of a WannaCry attack.

Sample WannaCry Attack Screen

6. **Equifax data breach (2017)**: A Massive Identity Theft Event between May and July of 2017, Equifax, one of the largest credit reporting agencies in the United States, suffered a major cybersecurity breach that exposed sensitive personal data on a staggering scale. The records of approximately 147.9 million Americans, along with 15.2 million individuals in the United Kingdom and nearly 19,000 Canadians, were compromised. The stolen information included names, Social Security numbers, birthdates, addresses, and in some cases, driver's license numbers, making it one of the most significant data breaches tied to identity theft in history.

Although Equifax identified the unauthorized access in late July 2017, the public was not informed until mid-September. This delay in disclosure drew sharp criticism from regulators, lawmakers, and the general public.

As part of a later agreement with the U.S. Federal Trade Commission (FTC) and other agencies, Equifax agreed to a settlement that included compensation options for those affected, such as free credit monitoring and reimbursement for certain expenses related to the breach.

In February 2020, the U.S. Department of Justice formally charged four members of China's People's Liberation Army (PLA) with conducting the cyberattack. Prosecutors accused the group of not only stealing consumer data but also obtaining valuable trade secrets. The Chinese government denied involvement in the breach.

The Equifax incident remains a landmark case in data security and privacy law, highlighting the vulnerabilities of large-scale data holders and the growing intersection of cybersecurity with geopolitics.

Diagram of Equifax Attack

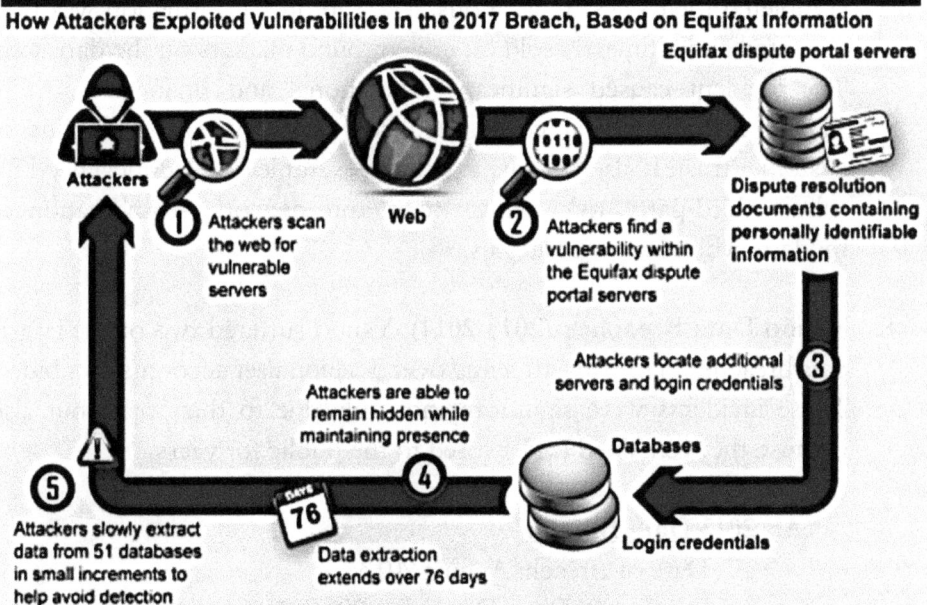

How Attackers Exploited Vulnerabilities in the 2017 Breach, Based on Equifax Information

Equifax dispute portal servers

Attackers

① Attackers scan the web for vulnerable servers

Web

② Attackers find a vulnerability within the Equifax dispute portal servers

Dispute resolution documents containing personally identifiable information

Attackers locate additional servers and login credentials ③

Attackers are able to remain hidden while maintaining presence

Databases

④

⑤ Attackers slowly extract data from 51 databases in small increments to help avoid detection

76 DAYS

Data extraction extends over 76 days

Login credentials

Source: GAO, based on information provided by Equifax. | GAO-18-559

United States Government Accountability Office

7. **Target Data Breach (2013):** In December 2013, during the peak of the holiday shopping season, Target Corporation experienced a major

cybersecurity breach that compromised millions of customer records. The intrusion exposed payment information for approximately 40 million debit and credit cards, along with personal details, such as names, phone numbers, and email addresses, of up to 70 million individuals.

The breach was traced back to compromised credentials belonging to a third-party service provider, Fazio Mechanical Services, a company that managed the heating and air-conditioning systems for Target. Attackers used these stolen login credentials to gain access to Target's internal network, a classic example of how vulnerabilities in vendor relationships can become entry points for larger cyberattacks.

Once inside, the attackers deployed malicious software onto the point-of-sale (POS) systems used in Target's physical retail stores. This malware was engineered to skim sensitive payment card data, including card numbers, expiration dates, and CVV security codes, as customers completed their sales transactions. The captured information was then extracted and ultimately sold on underground markets on the dark web. The incident caused significant reputational and financial harm to Target, including legal costs, regulatory scrutiny, and a decline in customer trust. It also became a defining example of the critical need for robust third-party risk management and network segmentation in modern cybersecurity strategies.

8. **Yahoo Data Breaches (2013-2014)**: Yahoo suffered two of the largest data breaches in history, affecting over 3 billion user accounts combined. These incidents were significant not only due to their scale but also because they remained undisclosed to the public for years.

   A. **2013 Data Breach**
   a) Date of Breach: August 2013
   b) Disclosure Date: December 2016
   c) Number of Accounts Affected: Originally believed to be 1 billion; later revised to 3 billion accounts in 2017.
   d) Data Compromised: Names, email addresses, telephone numbers, dates of birth, hashed passwords (using MD5), and possibly security questions and answers (both encrypted and unencrypted).

e) Cause: Yahoo attributed the breach to a "state-sponsored actor," though definitive attribution was never confirmed by independent cybersecurity firms.

B. **2014 Data Breach**
a) Date of Breach: Late 2014
b) Disclosure Date: September 2016
c) Number of Accounts Affected: About 500 million accounts
d) Data Compromised: Like the 2013 breach – names, emails, phone numbers, dates of birth, hashed passwords, and security questions and answers.
e) Suspected Actors: U.S. federal investigators later indicted four individuals, including two officers of Russia's FSB (Federal Security Service), in connection with this breach.

9. **Colonial Pipeline Ransomware Attack**: The Colonial Pipeline ransomware attack, conducted by the **DarkSide group**, was one of the most notable cybercrime incidents in 2021. **DarkSide**, a ransomware-as-a-service (RaaS) group, yes, there are hacking services for hire on the internet, was known for its sophisticated tactics and was hired to target Colonial Pipeline, a major fuel pipeline operator in the United States.

The attack took place in **May 2021** and had far-reaching consequences. The hackers gained unauthorized access to Colonial Pipeline's IT systems and deployed ransomware, which effectively encrypted critical data and systems, rendering them inaccessible. In response, the company took the precautionary measure of temporarily shutting down its pipeline operations to contain the breach and prevent further damage.

The pipeline, which spans over **5,500 miles** and supplies half of the fuel consumed on the East Coast of the United States, was offline for several days. The impact of the attack was significant, leading to fuel shortages across various states along the East Coast. Panic buying and hoarding exacerbated the situation, causing long lines at gas stations and price spikes. The disruption affected not only individual consumers but also businesses reliant on a steady fuel supply, including transportation companies, airlines, and emergency services.

In coordination with law enforcement agencies and cybersecurity experts, Colonial Pipeline worked to restore operations and mitigate the effects of the attack. They engaged with the DarkSide group and reportedly paid approximately **75 Bitcoin** (around **$4.4 million USD**) as ransom to obtain a decryption tool and restore their systems. While controversial, this decision was made to expedite the recovery process and minimize the impact on fuel distribution.

On **June 7, 2021,** the U.S. Department of Justice released a statement revealing its successful seizure of **63.7 Bitcoins** from the initial ransom payment. However, due to a decline in Bitcoin's trading price since the ransom was paid, the recovered Bitcoins were valued at only **$2.3 million**. The FBI was able to retrieve the Bitcoin by accessing the ransom account, although it did not disclose the method through which it obtained access.

David W. Evans

Warrant to Seize Stolen Assets

AO 109 (Rev. 11/13) Warrant to Seize Property Subject to Forfeiture

UNITED STATES DISTRICT
for the
Northern District of California

In the Matter of the Seizure of
(Briefly describe the property to be seized)
Application by the United States for a Seizure
Warrant for One Account for Investigation of 18
U.S.C. Section 981(a)(1)(A) and other offenses

Case No. 3:21-mj-70945-LB

WARRANT TO SEIZE PROPERTY SUBJECT TO FORFEITURE

To: Any authorized law enforcement officer

An application by a federal law enforcement officer or an attorney for the government requests that certain property located in the _____ Northern _____ District of _____ California _____ be seized as being subject to forfeiture to the United States of America. The property is described as follows:
Approximately 63.7 BTC (the "Subject Funds") accessible from the following cryptocurrency address (the "Subject Address")
XXXXXXXXXXXXX950klpjcawuy4uj39ym43hs6cfsegq

I find that the affidavit(s) and any recorded testimony establish probable cause to seize the property.

YOU ARE COMMANDED to execute this warrant and seize the property on or before   6/21/2021
(not to exceed 14 days)

☒ in the daytime 6:00 a.m. to 10:00 p.m.   ☐ at any time in the day or night because good cause has been established.

Unless delayed notice is authorized below, you must also give a copy of the warrant and a receipt for the property taken to the person from whom, or from whose premises, the property was taken, or leave the copy and receipt at the place where the property was taken.

An officer present during the execution of the warrant must prepare, as required by law, an inventory of any property seized and the officer executing the warrant must promptly return this warrant and a copy of the inventory to
_____ United States Magistrate Judge Laurel Beeler _____ .
(United States Magistrate Judge)

☐ Pursuant to 18 U.S.C. § 3103a(b), I find that immediate notification may have an adverse result listed in 18 U.S.C.
§ 2705 (except for delay of trial), and authorize the officer executing this warrant to delay notice to the person who, or whose property, will be searched or seized *(check the appropriate box)*
☐ for _____ days (not to exceed 30)   ☐ until, the facts justifying, the later specific date of _____

Date and time issued: 6/7/2021 9⁵⁰ᵃᵐ _____
Judge's signature

City and state: San Francisco CA 94102   Laurel Beeler, United States Magistrate Judge
Printed name and title

These incidents underscore the critical importance of robust cybersecurity measures across all technology systems to protect against significant financial and reputational damage.

Chapter 2

Why Would Cybercriminals Target Me

The typical technologies in homes today are the same three core types you see in larger organizations, except, most home users do not have the skills or resources to keep these technologies secure. Cybercriminals target all three layers. They are: **(1) networks, (2) devices, and (3) software.** We will explore each of these in detail throughout the following chapters, but here is a brief explanation of the core layers to help you identify what you may have in your home. Each one is a potential entry point for thieves, giving them access to steal your most valuable assets, or acquire the most confidential information you have. Some of the information they gain access to can be your personal contacts, in return giving them direct links to your financial accounts, business relationships, friends and relatives.

1. Networks

The most convenient and covert method cybercriminals use to attack your devices and software is through networks. They gain access to your systems from anywhere in the world through your Internet service or Wi-Fi while remaining hidden behind a cloak of anonymity. Cybercriminals can gain access to your accounts at your bank, your place of work, or the systems in your home from across the Internet. They can gain access to your home and your personal technologies via your internet service or Wi-Fi networks. These services are the core entry points into your home technologies. What they attack via these entrances is your devices, or the software on these devices. More on this below.

2. Devices

The list of technological devices in homes today can be extensive. Here is a list of the primary targets vulnerable to cybercriminals:

- **Smartphones**
- **Laptops & Desktop Computers**
- **Smart TVs**
- **Smart Home Assistants** (e.g., Amazon Echo, Google Home)
- **Wi-Fi Routers**
- **Security Cameras & Video Doorbells** (e.g., Ring, Nest)
- **Smart Thermostats** (e.g., Nest, Ecobee)
- **Smart Locks**
- **Smart Lighting Systems**
- **Baby Monitors**
- **Smart Appliances** (e.g., Refrigerators, Ranges, Washing Machines)
- **Printers**
- **Wearable Devices** (e.g., Smartwatches, Fitness Trackers)
- **Streaming Devices** (e.g., Roku, Apple TV, Amazon Fire Stick)
- **Home Automation Hubs** (e.g., SmartThings, HomeKit)
- **External Storage Devices** (e.g., NAS Drives)
- **Garage Door Openers** (e.g., Chamberlain MyQ, Genie Aladdin, iSmartGate)
- **Home Automation Systems (**e.g., Irrigation Systems, Smart Lighting)

3. Software

The list of software in homes today is also extensive. Every device listed above usually has several of the following software types, if not all three forms:

A) Operating Systems (OS)

The OS manages a device's hardware, software, memory, and processes. The most prevalent operating systems in use around a home today include:

1. **Windows OS** (Microsoft – Desktops, Laptops)
2. **iOS** (Apple Smartphones and iPads)
3. **Mac OS** (Apple Laptops)
4. **Android, Linux, and Chrome OS**: These are operating systems that power countless devices around the world and your home today, including:
   - **Smartphones**
   - **Tablets**
   - **Smart TVs**
   - **Streaming Devices**
   - **Smart Home Assistants**
   - **Wearables**
   - **Smart Home Appliances**
   - **Security Cameras & Video Doorbells**
   - **Smart Speakers**
   - **Automotive Systems**
   - **E-Readers**
   - **Game Consoles & Handheld Devices**
   - **Projectors**
   - **Garage Door Openers**

B) Firmware:
A form of Software embedded into hardware devices helping them function effectively. It typically comes already installed on the device when purchased but may need upgrading from time to time to remain safe and provide current functionality. Firmware upgrading is usually ignored by their owners because they were either unaware it exists, or they lack the knowledge required to maintain updates. Major strides have been made by the manufacturers in recent years to build automatic firmware updating features. You may have seen this feature on devices like Smart TV's, Smart

Watches' when they display a notice that the system will or has performed an upgrade. The best practice would be to enable automatic upgrading of firmware/software on every device in your home where available.

C) Applications

Applications (apps) are software programs that perform specific tasks on computers or devices. Improper user access or vulnerabilities in these apps can expose significant risks. We will delve into the cybersecurity concerns related to these in depth later.

Now that you have a better understanding of the technology landscape around your home, let us look at how cybercriminals attack each one.

Chapter 3

How Cybercriminals Target You

Social Engineering and Phishing Attacks

Social engineering is one of the most powerful tools cybercriminals use today. Roughly 57,000 Americans are scammed each day. Unlike traditional hacking that targets systems and software, social engineering exploits human behavior through deception and fraud, instead of trying to break through systems or crack difficult passwords. These cybercriminals deceive people into revealing sensitive information or performing actions that compromise security, sometimes without even realizing it. And just like that, you could be opening the door for crooks to exploit countless others, and/or steal millions of dollars.

A cybercriminal would not go through the hassle of identifying your vulnerable systems and then breaching them if they can simply trick you into inviting them in and giving them total control of your systems. It is no wonder this method has become one of the most popular attack strategies in recent years. The vast majority of an individuals or home cybersecurity breaches are due to user actions or neglect, not technology failure. And most of these attacks are performed on weak cloud account or PC protection. Here is a breakdown of the likely causes:

Source of Breach	Estimated Likelihood
User behavior (phishing, weak passwords)	70–90%
Unpatched/vulnerable software on PC	10–20%
Home router/network misconfiguration	5–10%
Smart home devices (IoT)	2–5%
Malicious insider or physical access	<1%

So based on most common attack risks, let us start with user behavior. Below are some of the most common forms of social engineering attacks and how they can impact you:

Phishing: Phishing is a classic example, where attackers trick people into giving away sensitive information like passwords, credit card details, or Social Security numbers. They do this by sending fake emails, texts, or counterfeit messages that appear to be from trusted sources, such as your bank, a government agency, or even companies like Amazon, Google, or eBay. Both phishing and other social engineering attacks rely on psychological manipulation, preying on trust, fear, urgency, or curiosity to get you to act without thinking twice.

An example of a Phishing attack would be the use of an email that looks like it is from a reputable company like Amazon saying your account has been frozen and asks you to log in through a link provided in the email asking you to update or validate your account. The link, however, takes you to a **fake Amazon site**, where criminals collect your username and password credentials when you login. Or the email requires you to call a phone number that is not a legitimate Amazon phone number.

Sample Amazon Phishing Attack

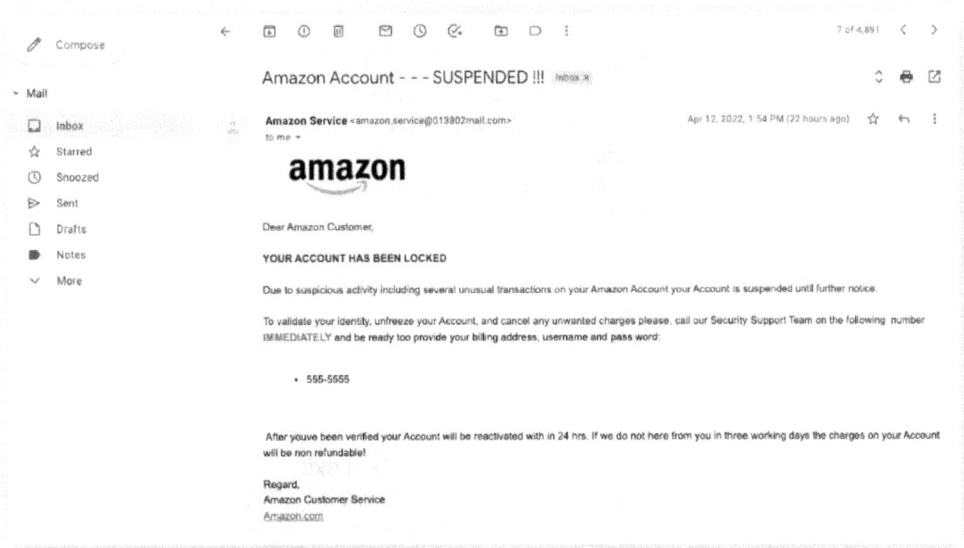

A safer method to validate whether this is a fake or real communication, is to visit amazon.com, or look up the real Amazon phone number and check your account status and notifications. If your account is locked, or if Amazon requires an account validation or recovery request to update your account status, you will know it was legitimate communication. The key is to use information directly from the source service provider and never provide information through a random request.

Smishing: Is a Fraudulent SMS (Short Message Service) or better known as text message asking the recipient to click on a malicious link, or/or provides a deceitful request attempting criminal behavior towards the result of a compromise. As you can see from the following example asking you to both, click on a link that is not the legitimate web address for USPS, and ask you to supply personal information like your zip code. You might be tempted to think your zip code would be harmless to supply because it is available through many sources, but what if a cybercriminal in another country had your credit card information and all they were missing to use it was your zip code to validate purchases online or at a gas pump for example. See the following:

Sample Smishing Attack

Today 6:37 AM

U.S. Post: You have a USPS parcel being cleared, due to the detection of an invalid zip code address, the parcel can not be cleared, the parcel is temporarily detained, please confirm the zip
code address information in the link
within 24 hours.

https://i.usertrackssb.top/us

(Please reply with a Y, then exit the text message and open it again to activate the link, or copy the link into your Safari browser and open it)
Have a great day from the USPS team!

\+   iMessage

Vishing: Voice phishing scams involve attackers posing as customer service representatives or government agents. These attacks are often tailored to the victim, making them convincing and difficult to detect. Many identity theft victims are not immediately aware of the theft. It can take months or even years to discover that a criminal has been using their identity.

Vishing calls might come from an actual person or use automated robocall technology or some combination of both. The caller may know nothing about you, or they may provide information such as your address or even the last four digits of your Social Security number to win your trust. The best practice is to NEVER answer calls from a phone number or someone you do not recognize, or a call you are not expecting. If it is important, they will leave a voicemail message, and you can call them back. Just answering a call and saying something could be enough to record your voice and then utilize tools like Artificial Intelligence (AI) to develop your voice to use maliciously. Say to convince a friend, co-worker, or financial institution to perform fraud and costly attacks.

In every attempt, there will be a request for more information. Here are a few general vishing categories:

- **Solving a problem with your account.** A caller, purportedly from your bank or another organization you do business with, explains that there is a problem with your account access, a payment you recently made, suspicious transactions or perhaps a refund you are owed. The caller requests information, such as a change to existing payment instructions, your access code or account number, to resolve the issue.
- **A demand for payment.** Scammers may pretend to work for government agencies, such as the IRS or the FBI, or as employees at collection agencies or other third parties. They may tell you that you owe money and must pay immediately or be fined or even arrested. These scams may also include text messages from the scammer to make their request look legitimate.
- **Technical support.** Unsolicited calls or voicemails that refer to legitimate companies may advise you to use a phone number to contact a customer support number to resolve a problem with technical services or devices. Remember, reputable companies will never ask you for your account details unless you call them first. These scammers can be very convincing. Some offer solutions to a problem (such as your software needs to be upgraded). They offer software support to help secure your system. *You should never give out personal or company information to an unsolicited caller.* To be safe, you can always verify the entity and call back if they are a reputable company. If they are truly a company that performs cybersecurity, they should understand this. I have kicked an FBI agent auditing our operations out of my building before, because he could not provide adequate identification. He did not like it but understood due to inadequate documentation.
- **Enrollment Scams.** Some cybercriminals pose as representatives of government programs, such as the Social Security Administration or Medicare, and try to collect personal or financial information under the guise of helping you enroll or receive payments. Criminals have also exploited the Small Business Association's Paycheck Protection Program

to target business owners seeking loans.

- **Deepfake AI Calls.** A newer method of social engineering that has developed in recent years is Deepfake AI Calls. Deepfake AI calls use advanced artificial intelligence to manipulate or synthesize voices in a way that convincingly mimics real people. This technology can produce audio clips or live conversations that sound almost indistinguishable from the real person it is imitating. While deepfake audio has potential applications in entertainment and education, it also raises significant ethical, security, and privacy concerns. A snippet of a person's voice can be captured from social media or from a phone call and used to reproduce an entire vocabulary of a person. Have you ever answered a call from a phone number you did not recognize and said something, and then they hung up? The AI generated voice is then used via a call to someone the person knows to request help, information, or money in the end.

- **Collecting an award or exclusive offer.** An old scam that is frequently recycled, the vishing caller informs the recipient that they have won a contest or can cash in a limited time offer of goods or services. Personal or payment information is then requested.

If you are already using the services they are speaking of, the recommended solution would be going directly through their application, web portal or call them directly to validate your status. Never use a link provided by an unknown or unsolicited source.

Software Exploitation

Malware is an umbrella term used to describe a variety of malicious software designed to disrupt, damage, or gain unauthorized access to systems. Malware infects devices through malicious links or files, allowing criminals to steal data or control your system remotely.

Examples of Malware:
- **Viruses**: Programs that attach themselves to legitimate software and spread when users run the infected software.

- **Trojans**: Malware disguised as legitimate software, providing hackers with remote access to your device.
- **Spyware**: Software that secretly watches your activities, collecting sensitive information such as passwords and banking credentials.
- **Ransomware:** Is a specific and particularly dangerous form of malware that locks your files or data and demands payment for their release. Ransomware attacks are becoming more sophisticated, while some attackers even target families by threatening to release personal photos, videos, or financial information to the public. Attackers encrypt your data to the point that it becomes unusable and demand a ransom before granting access. This payment is typically requested in the form of Bitcoin or other cryptocurrencies, making it untraceable and protected. Recent ransomware campaigns go beyond data encryption; they also threaten to leak personal information online if the ransom is not paid. Families have lost irreplaceable or compromising photos, videos, and personal documents due to ransomware attacks. Additionally, paying the ransom does not guarantee that access will be restored, and that attackers will not retain control of your files and return for further compensation.

Example:
A user receives an email attachment labeled as an invoice. Upon opening the attachment, ransomware is triggered, locking their files, and demanding a ransom of $500 to restore access. If no backup is available, the individual must either pay the ransom or risk permanently losing their data. In the U.S., some estimates suggest only a small fraction (possibly under 5%) of reported cybercrimes result in an arrest, let alone a conviction. And with the largest portion of these attacks originating internationally, changes of conviction are even less.

Once malware infects your system, attackers can gain access to emails, personal documents, and stored passwords, or use your computer to perform further damage. By using your systems, they can make all this additional damage appear as if you performed it.

Risks on Public Wi-Fi and Smart Devices

Public Wi-Fi networks at coffee shops, airports, or hotels may seem convenient, but these networks are often unsecured and notorious for their security risks. Attackers on public Wi-Fi networks can perform **man-in-the-middle (MitM)** attacks, intercepting your traffic and stealing passwords and other sensitive data. Cybercriminals position themselves on network communications between two parties to steal data in transmission.

Smart devices, such as thermostats, security cameras, smart TVs, and voice-activated devices like Alexa, Google Home, or Nest, can provide easy access to your home network if the software on these systems is not kept up-to-date or configured with weak passwords.

SECURING YOUR DIGITAL LIFE

Chapter 4

Building Strong Passwords

Creating strong passwords is essential and remains one of the most effective first steps in protecting your personal accounts from unauthorized access. A strong password should be **unique, long,** and **difficult to guess,** not just by people, but also by computers and even artificial intelligence (AI). Let me explain.

Why the Login Process is Still So Frustrating

Despite years of progress, the industry has largely failed to simplify the login process or create a universal replacement for passwords. Instead, we are left with:

- Conflicting password requirements across different platforms
- Outdated rules enforced by some providers.
- Complex and inconsistent password management expectations

When you consider the average household now interacts with dozens of online services, this fragmentation becomes even more overwhelming.

There is a clear disconnect between:

- **Standards organizations** work to create secure, user-friendly guidance.
- **Service providers** are struggling to balance usability with security.
- **Everyday users** manage dozens of logins, each with different rules.

Unlike the simple 4-digit PIN that became the global standard for ATMs, no equivalent exists for online accounts.

Current best practices promoted by cybersecurity authorities **emphasize length and uniqueness** (e.g., 12–16+ characters), rather than outdated complexity rules. However, many service providers still require only **8-character passwords** with a forced mix of letters, numbers, and symbols, often resulting in passwords that are both hard to remember and easier to crack.

As a result, users frequently:

- Choose weak but easy-to-remember passwords.
- Reuse passwords across multiple accounts.
- Write them down or store them insecurely.

A Shift Toward Simpler, Smarter Security

Simplifying the login process can directly improve password security. Forward-thinking organizations are addressing this challenge with **passwordless authentication** solutions.

Groups like the FIDO Alliance have developed tools such as:

- Passkeys
- Biometric authentication (fingerprint, face ID)

- Hardware security tokens

These technologies are already built into many modern devices and platforms, yet adoption is still evolving. For now, passwords remain necessary in most cases.

Bottom Line:

There is no single, universal login system in place today.

So, in this chapter, I will provide:

- A breakdown of the most effective techniques currently available for managing passwords securely.
- Data on what makes a password strong in today's threat landscape.
- Practical guidance and recommendations for creating strong passwords and simplifying your login process, based on real-world conditions and current tools.

Characteristics of a Strong Password

- **Length:** At least 8 characters. The longer the password, the stronger it is and exponentially harder to crack. *Aim for 12–16 characters for strong passwords or sensitive information.*
- **Complexity:** Include a mix of uppercase and lowercase letters, numbers, and special symbols (e.g., @, #, %, !). *Making this a routine for your password generation will typically meet most service providers' minimum standards.*
- **Unpredictability:** Avoid dictionary words or easily guessable patterns (like "Password123", "LetMeIn" or "ChangeMe").
- **Avoid Personal Information:** Do not use personal details such as birthdays, names, pet names, street address or phone numbers. Avoid information that can be found online or social media like your high school's name or where you were born if it is the same city, you currently live.
- **Use Passphrases:** A combination of random words such as "MyLaptopDances3TimesDaily! " can be easier to remember but still secure.

I know these recommendations from the standards authorities are daunting.

So, to help simplify your passwords and keep them strong, my recommendation is to use passwords generated by a password generation tool or a password manager. If you are trying to keep it simple, follow the lead of most service providers with the minimum login criteria of 8 characters made up of upper and lower case, numbers, and symbols. Based on current measurements, it would take a hacker roughly 164 years to crack a password constructed with these criteria. I would recommend backing this up with one of the compromised login monitoring options mentioned in this book. **There is more on this later.**

Tips to Keep Passwords Safe

- **Never Reuse Passwords:** Each account should have a unique password to prevent a breach from affecting multiple accounts.
- **Avoid Writing Passwords Down:** Use a password manager or encrypted storage if you need to record them.
- **Enable Two-Factor Authentication (2FA):** 2FA adds an extra layer of security, such as sending a code to your phone.

How Hackers Crack Passwords

As you have probably noticed, entering the wrong password too many times usually triggers a temporary lockout. Modern systems enforce **rate-limiting,** for example, blocking further attempts after X failures per minute, to keep attackers from guessing passwords indefinitely.

Here is the critical part: most criminals do not hammer the live login page. Instead, they launch **offline password attacks,** which become possible after the large-scale data breaches you hear about in the news (e.g., "Company X" was hacked) and the data and passwords of their users has been stolen.

How stolen credentials are weaponized
1. A hacker breaches a company's system and steals user credentials.
2. Passwords are rarely stored in plain text; they are usually **hashed** (a one-way cryptographic transformation that is difficult to reverse).
3. Back at their own machines, free from lockout limits, the attacker unleashes tools such as **Hashcat** or **John the Ripper** to crack those hashed passwords.

4. These tools can test **billions of password guesses per second** by combining:
   • Huge dictionaries of words and phrases. These are not just made up of words you would find in a standard dictionary. They are far more comprehensive and tailored to common password creation habits
   • Lists of previously leaked passwords
   • Rule-based tweaks (e.g., changing "a" to "@" or adding numbers)
5. Once cracked, the passwords are reused directly or sold on the dark web.

Because offline cracking faces no rate limits, brute-force and rules-based methods are alarmingly effective, often leading to account takeovers before victims realize anything is wrong.

Why password strength matters

To illustrate, consider eight-character passwords and the time it takes in today's environment to compromise:

- **All numbers**: cracked instantly.
- **All lowercase letters**: ~3 weeks
- **Mixed upper/lowercase + numbers**: ~15 years
- **Upper/lowercase + numbers + symbols**: ~164 years

(Actual times can vary with the attacker's hardware and will shorten as computing power increases.)

The good news

Creating and remembering strong passwords does not have to be painful. Modern password managers can generate and store complex passwords for you, and setup usually takes just a few minutes. With one master password and a little practice, anyone can stay far better protected.

Remember, stronger passwords are dramatically safer, but do not eliminate, the chance of being hacked. That is why backing up your data and having a solid recovery plan are just as important. We will cover those topics in later chapters.

Table Showing How Long it Takes to Crack Passwords

Time it takes a hacker to brute force your password in 2025

Hardware: 12 x RTX 5090 | Password hash: bcrypt (10)

Number of Characters	Numbers Only	Lowercase Letters	Upper and Lowercase Letters	Numbers, Upper and Lowercase Letters	Numbers, Upper and Lowercase Letters, Symbols
4	Instantly	Instantly	Instantly	Instantly	Instantly
5	Instantly	Instantly	57 minutes	2 hours	4 hours
6	Instantly	46 minutes	2 days	6 days	2 weeks
7	Instantly	20 hours	4 months	1 year	2 years
8	Instantly	3 weeks	15 years	62 years	164 years
9	2 hours	2 years	791 years	3k years	11k years
10	1 day	40 years	41k years	238k years	803k years
11	1 weeks	1k years	2m years	14m years	56m years
12	3 months	27k years	111m years	917m years	3bn years
13	3 years	705k years	5bn years	56bn years	275bn years
14	28 years	18m years	300bn years	3tn years	19tn years
15	284 years	477m years	15tn years	218tn years	1qd years
16	2k years	12bn years	812tn years	13qd years	94qd years
17	28k years	322bn years	42qd years	840qd years	6qn years
18	284k years	8tn years	2qn years	52qn years	463qn years

⊞ **Hive Systems**

Read more and download at hivesystems.com/password

More information can be found on this at:
https://www.hivesystems.com/blog/are-your-passwords-in-the-green?utm_source=tabletext

Using Password Managers

Password managers are tools designed to generate, store, and manage complex passwords for multiple accounts, reducing the risk associated with weak or reused passwords. This technology is rapidly improving, so I would recommend searching for an updated list for the top PW Managers currently, and information on how to use them if you are not already knowledgeable about the technology.

Benefits of Password Managers

- **Single Source:** All your passwords are kept in one location.
- **Generate Strong, Random Passwords:** Password managers can create long and complex passwords that are hard to crack.
- **Single Master Password:** You only need to remember the one master password to your password manager.
- **Autofill Capability:** Password managers can automatically fill in your login credentials and passwords for websites and apps.
- **Encrypted Storage:** Password managers store credentials in an encrypted database, ensuring only the user with the master password can access them.
- **Easy Access:** Some give free access (maybe limited) or are built into your device manufacture.

Types of Password Managers

- **Cloud-Based Managers:** Store passwords on secure servers and sync across devices.
    - Examples: 1Password, NordPass, Dashlane, RoboForm, Proton Pass, Keeper Password Manager & Digital Vault.
- **Local-Based Managers:** Store passwords locally on your device.
    - Examples: KeePass, NordPass.
- **Browser-Based Managers:** Integrated into web browsers for convenience but may lack advanced security features.
    - **Examples:** Chrome Password Manager, Firefox Lockwise.

How to Use a Password Manager Effectively

- **Create a Strong Master Password:** The master password should follow strong password principles and be unique.
- **Enable 2FA on the Password Manager:** This adds multiple layers of security further protecting your stored credentials.
- **Regularly Update Passwords:** The Cybersecurity and Infrastructure Security Agency (CISA) recommends changing passwords primarily when there's evidence of a compromise or suspicion of unauthorized

access.

- **Review Security Reports:** Many password managers and anti-virus software packages provide reports showing weak or reused passwords and compromised accounts. Access to these reports is different depending on the applications you are using, but they can be extremely helpful and sometimes very revealing. I would highly recommend using these reports. If you do not already have access to one, I would highly recommend looking into an application or service that will provide them.

Risks and How to Mitigate Them

Single Point of Failure: If someone gains access to your master password, they can access all your accounts.
Mitigation: Use 2FA, strong master passwords, and biometrics (where available).
Cloud Breaches: Hackers may target cloud-based password managers.
Mitigation: Use managers with zero-knowledge encryption, meaning even the company cannot access your data.

Simplified Login Strategy for Everyday Users

The following are the Password Use Recommendations promised above. Now that you have a good picture of strong password creation and the range of login options available, let us look at recommendations and a plan for your use going forward. After initial setup, this plan will more than likely allow you to login to most of your Apps and Services without the need to remember or enter passwords in most cases. This will expedite and simplify your logins substantially. You may have to read details of some of these options in other chapters of this book.

> **Use this progression:** Start at the top with the most secure and convenient method. If the method is not available for a particular login, move to the next option.

> **Option 1: Use a Passwordless Login (FIDO2 / Passkeys)**
> **Use this if the service supports it.**
> - **What it is:** Login using your **fingerprint, Face ID, or device PIN**, without needing to remember or use a password.

- **How to do it**: Enable **Passkey login** or **"Sign in with device"** (like Apple, Google, or Microsoft).
- **Where it is supported**: Google, Microsoft, Apple, many mobile Apps, password managers, and some banking sites.
- **Most secure** and **easiest to use** once set up.

If FIDO2 or passkeys are not available, move to Option 2.

Option 2: Use a Password Manager + MFA (Multi Factor Authentication) *Discussed in detail later.*
Use this for websites and apps that still require passwords.

- **Use a Password Manager** (like 1Password, Bitwarden, or iCloud Keychain) to:
  - Generate long, unique passwords.
  - Autofill them for you on websites and apps
  - Sync across devices securely.
- **Enable MFA (Multi-Factor Authentication)** for important accounts (email, banking, cloud).

If you cannot use a password manager, move to Option 3.

Option 3: Use Strong, Memorable Passphrases + MFA.
If you must manage passwords yourself, make them long and simple to remember.

- Use a **passphrase** instead of a password:
  Example: RedPizzaChairBanana$22.
- Still **enable MFA** where possible.
- **Write down backup codes,** recovery keys or passwords and store them in a safe place like a vault, not your office or where they can be easily found. Criminals are crafty and know the typical hiding places.

If MFA is not available, move to Option 4.

Option 4: Use Unique, Strong Passwords at Minimum
When limited to just passwords, make them count.

- Use a different password for each account.
- Make each password strong based on recommended standards supplied earlier.

- Use a Password generator to develop or recommend strong passwords. Many applications or web browsers provide this feature. Another good option for password generation or just checking one that you have created is:

Trusted Password Generation Tools

These tools help you create strong, random, and secure passwords or passphrases:

1. Bitwarden Password Generator

- https://bitwarden.com/password-generator
- Free, open-source, customizable
- Supports random passwords *and* memorable passphrases.

2. 1Password Strong Password Generator

- https://1password.com/password-generator
- Create random or memorable passwords.
- Strong privacy practices

3. LastPass Password Generator

- https://www.lastpass.com/password-generator
- Easy-to-use, customizable for length and character type
- Option for pronounceable passwords

Password Strength Checkers

These tools evaluate how strong your password is, based on structure, length, and breach history.

1. Have I Been Pwned – Pwned Passwords

- https://haveibeenpwned.com/Passwords
- Checks if your password has appeared in known data breaches.
- Does not store your password; uses partial hash lookup.

2. Kaspersky Password Strength Checker

- https://password.kaspersky.com
- Visualizes how long it would take to crack your password.

- Avoid entering your **real** passwords, use a close variation.

3. PasswordMonster
- https://www.passwordmonster.com
- Gives detailed strength analysis.
- Estimates crack time and security level.

Conclusion

Using strong passwords along with a password manager is essential for modern digital security. A password manager ensures you do not have to remember or reuse passwords, while strong passwords keep individual accounts secure. Implementing two-factor authentication on top of these practices will further safeguard your information.

Chapter 5

Multi-Factor Authentication (MFA)

What is Multi-Factor Authentication (MFA)?

Multi-Factor Authentication (MFA) - usually requires at least two of the following three types of authentication factors:

1. **Something You Know:**
   o Passwords, PINs, security questions.
2. **Something You Have:**
   o Physical devices like smartphones, smart cards, or hardware tokens.
   o One-time passcodes (OTPs) are sent via SMS, email, or an

authentication app.
3. **Something You Are**:
   o Biometric identifiers, such as fingerprints, facial recognition, or retina scans.

You may be unknowingly using this service in at least one-way today if this sounds familiar. Say you are logging into your bank or another service.
1. You enter your username and password (**something you know**). Your username and password are something you pre-established with the bank when you set up the account. So, they have a high trust that it is something you know.
2. The app sends a prompt or requires a code sent to your phone (**something you have**). Your mobile phone number would also have been established with the bank when you set up your account and/or activated MFA service. Your bank then has a reasonable trust that they are sending this code to your personal cell phone.
3. You use Facial ID or fingerprint to unlock the app or approve the login (**something you are**). These two items are very personal, hard to duplicate and trustworthy.

For a cybercriminal to gain access to all three of these is far less likely than just acquiring one of them. This is why MFA is much more secure than just a password or code.

This is MFA. Multi-Factor Authentication (MFA) and Two-Factor Authentication (2FA) are security mechanisms designed to protect accounts and systems by requiring multiple forms of verification before access is gained. MFA and 2FA are related, but they are not the same thing. Here is a quick breakdown: Here is how they differ and where they overlap:

Definitions
1. **Two-Factor Authentication (2FA):**
   • A specific type of MFA that uses exactly **two** distinct types of authentication factors.
2. **Multi-Factor Authentication (MFA):**
   • A broader term that requires two or more distinct factors.

- MFA can include 2FA but is not limited to just two factors; it could require three or more layers of verification.

Key Differences

Aspect	2FA	MFA
Number of Factors	Always **two factors**.	**Two or more factors**.
Complexity	Simpler setup and usage.	More robust and secure but potentially more complex.
Use Cases	Commonly used for personal accounts (e.g., email, social media).	Often used for high-security environments like enterprise systems or financial institutions.
Examples	Password + One-Time Password (OTP).	Password + OTP + Biometric (e.g., fingerprint).

MFA is sometimes used to describe the methods in general sometimes. It is recommended that you set up at least 2FA on all critical accounts, including banking apps, email, social platforms, and especially your smartphone. While MFA is not foolproof, it significantly reduces the risk of unauthorized access. **Risk = Impact × Probability.** According to the leading technology manufactures and cybersecurity companies, MFA reduces the risk of compromise by over 99% across the general population and by over 98% in cases involving leaked credentials. That is drastic improvement above standard single-login services.

Why MFA is Essential for Security

Protection Against Password Breaches

- **Passwords Alone Are Vulnerable:** Weak, reused, or stolen passwords are common targets in cyberattacks. When passwords are stolen, they can be sold on the Internet to countless cybercriminals and used endlessly. MFA ensures that even if a password is compromised, it is virtually useless without the second authentication factor.

Mitigates Phishing Attacks

- **Phishing campaigns** try to trick users into sharing their credentials. However, with MFA, even stolen passwords are often useless without the second authentication factor.

Limits the Impact of Data Breaches

- If attackers obtain login credentials through data breaches, MFA prevents them from accessing other services tied to the same password.

Reduces Risks from Social Engineering

- Attackers often use psychological manipulation to trick individuals into revealing passwords or other credentials. MFA adds a technical barrier that reduces the effectiveness of these techniques.

Secures Remote Access and Online Transactions

- With the rise of remote work and online banking, MFA ensures that unauthorized access attempts are blocked, even if credentials are compromised through phishing or brute force attacks.

Types of MFA Solutions

One-Time Passwords (OTPs)

An OTP is a security mechanism that generates a unique, temporary password or code that can only be used once, usually within a brief time window. OTPs are widely used to enhance security for authentication processes, typically as part of two-factor authentication (2FA) or multi-factor authentication (MFA). You may recognize these methods. They are extremely popular.

- **Delivered via SMS or Email:** Delivered to a user's registered phone number or email address.
- **App-Generated OTPs:** Time-based One-Time Passwords (TOTP) are generated by apps like Google Authenticator, Microsoft Authenticator, or Authy. These codes typically expire within 30-60 seconds. If you are unsuccessful in acquiring access in this timeframe, you are required to establish a new OTP.
- These are generated based on the current time and a shared secret key.

Push Notifications

- A notification is sent to a smartphone app (like Duo or Okta) asking the user to approve or deny a login request. This is a convenient and secure method, as it also allows users to detect unauthorized access attempts.

Hardware Security Keys

- Physical devices, such as **YubiKey** or **Feitian tokens**, must be plugged into a USB port or tapped on a phone with NFC. These keys are highly secure and resistant to phishing.

Biometrics

- Authentication using **fingerprints, face recognition**, or **iris scanning**. Often integrated with devices (like smartphones or laptops) and offers a fast, user-friendly experience.

Adaptive or Risk-Based MFA

- **Context-aware systems** are a smarter, more dynamic form of multi-factor authentication that analyze risk factors (such as your IP address, device type, or location) to determine if additional authentication is required. For example, logging in from a new location or a device you never used before may trigger MFA and additional security credentials, while locations you have login from before or known devices might bypass requiring additional information. You may have seen this when you are prompted at a login if this device is trusted (One you know about), so the device and/or location can be added to your approved list. You may also receive a code to approve, or notification that a new device is using your login credentials.

How MFA Works in Practice

1. **Login Attempt:** The user enters their username and password.
2. **Second-Factor Prompt:** If the password is correct, the system asks for a second form of authentication, like facial recognition or fingerprint.
3. **Authentication Verified:** If the second factor is verified (e.g., OTP or biometric scan), the user gains access to the system.

Best Practices for Implementing MFA

Enable MFA on Critical Accounts: Focus on protecting accounts related to:

- Financial services (banks, credit cards, etc.)
- Email accounts (as these can be used to reset other passwords)

- Social media accounts (to prevent identity theft or account takeovers)
- Cloud services and work accounts (to secure sensitive information)

I recommend using MFA on all accounts where the experience is user-friendly. Let us face it, it is much easier for a user to use facial recognition or a fingerprint on their phone than to remember and enter a lengthy, complex password.

Use Authentication Apps over SMS:
As we learned earlier, SMS is a (Short Message Service), and the typical form of texting used today. SMS-based codes can be intercepted through **SIM swapping** attacks, where hackers take control of your phone number. **SIM swapping** (also called SIM hijacking or SIM swap fraud) is a type of cyberattack where a hacker tricks a mobile carrier into transferring your phone number to a SIM card they control. Once they have your number, they can receive your calls and texts, including 2FA codes, giving them access to your sensitive accounts. There is more on this later. Authentication Apps like **Google Authenticator** or **Microsoft Authenticator** offer more secure alternatives.

Combine Biometrics with Other Factors:
Relying solely on biometrics is not foolproof, biometric data can be spoofed or stolen. Combining it with another factor (like a PIN) improves security. This is considered layering security. The thought is to build many layers like an onion and develop multiple obstacles between you and threats.

Train Family Members:
Make sure family members understand the importance of MFA and how to use it properly. This can make application and service logins much easier and adds much greater protection. Also, awareness of phishing can help mitigate risks.

Challenges and Limitations of MFA
User Convenience vs. Security:
Some users may find MFA inconvenient, especially if it requires multiple steps. Adaptive MFA can help strike a balance by triggering additional factors only when necessary. Selecting 'remember this device,' if available, can also help so that extra steps are not required every time. Remember, selecting 'remember this device,' should only be used on a computer you own and not, for example, a

public kiosk in a hotel or airport. As this is saying, it is ok for this computer to bypass some security measures in the future. You should only apply this feature to computers/devices personally to you or your home.

Device Dependency:
Users may lose their phones or security tokens, which can lock them out of their accounts temporarily. Many services offer **backup codes** or alternative recovery methods to address this. Many phones or devices have a find my device feature. This is an excellent feature if set up ahead of time. Some of these tools can not only help you find your device, but they can also give you the ability to lock your device, and in some instances delete and remove all personal and sensitive data. Including passcode keys.

Phishing-Resistant MFA Still Needed:
Although Basic MFA methods (like OTPs sent via SMS) are effective and much better than a single password, they can be susceptible to phishing attacks. There are more secure methods, such as **hardware keys** or **FIDO2 authentication**, which are recommended for high-risk accounts. There is more on this below.

MFA in Today's Cybersecurity Landscape

With the increasing frequency and sophistication of cyberattacks, MFA is no longer a luxury, it is a necessity. Many companies, governments, and online services are now mandating MFA to reduce the risks of unauthorized access. In fact, major tech companies like Google, Apple, and Microsoft have begun implementing **passwordless authentication** options, such as **passkeys**, which rely on biometrics or device-based security. In fact, **passwordless authentication** is more secure and easier to use. For this reason, it is quickly becoming the future of logins. You can use these technologies to login to many services and accounts like Google or Microsoft. Here are some of the most popular forms of passwordless authentication used in industry today.

Hardware keys: Hardware keys (also known as security keys or hardware tokens) are physical devices used to provide secure access to systems or accounts, usually as part of multi-factor authentication (MFA). This can be performed as easy as saving a hardware key on a USB stick. The following are some of the most popular devices used today:

- **USB -** USB stands for Universal Serial Bus, it is standard technology that allows computers and electronic devices to communicate and transfer data and power through a cable or port.

    Example of using a USB device to login passwordless to Google -Registration (one-time setup) – When you use your device for its first use with a service like Google, when you have completed the one-time registration, the device creates a unique public/private key pair. The public key is sent to the service, the private key stays on your USB device. You have now registered your USB-based FIDO2 security key with your account.

    o Go to: https://accounts.google.com on your laptop or desktop.
    o Enter your email address and click "Next."
    o Instead of asking for a password, Google prompts: "Insert your security key to continue"
    o You plug your USB security key into the computer.
    o Enter a PIN if required.
    o The USB key cryptographically signs the login challenge.
    o Google verifies it with the public key it stored during setup.
    o You are logged in; no password is needed.

- **Near Field Communication (NFC) -** NFC device refers to any device that uses Near Field Communication (NFC) technology to securely exchange data over short distances, typically a few centimeters. YubiKey, Smartphones and Access Cards & Badges are some you may know. Here is one example of how it works.

    Example of using NFC to perform Apple Pay - When you hold your iPhone or Apple Watch near a contactless payment terminal:
    o NFC establishes a secure connection between your device and the terminal.
    o You confirm the transaction with: Face ID, Touch ID, or your device passcode.
    o Apple Pay sends a tokenized version of your payment info (not your real card number) to the terminal.
    o The payment goes through securely and quickly, usually in under a second.

- **Bluetooth-enabled device -** Bluetooth-enabled devices can function as a "second factor" in the login processes. Instead of receiving a text or using an app, you physically connect or tap the key to authenticate yourself. Here is one example of how it works.

> **Example of using a Bluetooth-enabled device to login passwordless to your Google Account -** You're logging into your Google Account on a laptop. Instead of using a password or a physical security key, you are using your Bluetooth-enabled smartphone.
> o You go to https://accounts.google.com on your laptop. After entering your email, Google prompts:
> "Use your phone to sign in."
> o Your phone and laptop communicate via Bluetooth to establish a secure link.
> o You get a notification on your smartphone:
> "Are you trying to sign in?"
> o You approve the sign-in using:
> Face ID or fingerprint or your phone's screen lock PIN
> o The phone cryptographically signs the login request using a private key stored securely on the device. You are logged in, password-free and phishing-resistant.

FIDO: FIDO stands for Fast IDentity Online. It is a set of open standards developed by the FIDO Alliance to make online authentication more secure and user-friendly, without relying on passwords. FIDO is your friend. While the cybersecurity industry has been promoting stronger, lengthy, more difficult passwords to remember, the goal of FIDO is to go passwordless, and make login easier and safer. It is the future of authentication services. It enables passwordless logins to websites, apps, and services using strong public key cryptography.

Here is how the FIDO Login Works:
Registration (one-time setup) – When you use your device for its first use with a service like Google or Microsoft, you register your device (phone, security key, etc.) with a service. This is performed on the services you plan to use, like Google

or Microsoft. When you have completed the one-time registration, the device creates a unique public/private key pair. The public key is sent to the service, the private key stays on your device.

Example of using FIDO2 to login passwordless to your Google account
- You previously set up a FIDO2 security key by registering a device (like your smartphone) with Google as a FIDO2 authenticator.
    - You go to the site, for example Google.
    - Enter your email address and click "Next."
    - Instead of prompting a password, Google says:
    - "Use your security key to continue"
    - Choose your FIDO2 authenticator.
    - Google should detect a Bluetooth-linked smartphone.
    - Your authenticator will ask for a second factor: Fingerprint scan/Face ID/Device PIN
    - Once verified, your device signs a cryptographic challenge.
    - Google checks the digital signature with the stored public key.
    - You are logged in, no password used.

Conclusion
MFA is a critical layer of defense in today's interconnected world. It ensures that even if one authentication factor is compromised, whether through phishing, brute force, or a data breach, your accounts and sensitive information remain protected. Although there are some challenges associated with MFA, the benefits far outweigh the inconveniences. By implementing MFA wherever possible, you enhance your personal and organizational security, significantly reducing the likelihood of unauthorized access.

Chapter 6

Safe Internet Browsing Practices

🔑

As more of our daily lives take place online, practicing safe browsing is essential to protect against threats such as malware, phishing, and data breaches. By following safe internet practices, you can safeguard your personal information, avoid scams, and maintain privacy while online.

Use a Secure Browser

- **Keep Your Browser Updated:** Regular updates include security patches that address vulnerabilities.
- **Enable Security Features:** Modern browsers (like Google Chrome, Firefox, Edge, and Safari) offer settings for:

- o Pop-up blocking
- o Do Not Track requests.
- o **Safe browsing tools** (e.g., Google Safe Browsing warns about malicious sites).
- **Avoid Using Unsupported Browsers:** Older browsers may have unpatched security vulnerabilities, therefore putting you in danger of harm.

Use Secure Websites Only: Why It is Crucial for Safe Browsing

When you browse the internet, the security of your information depends on how that information is transmitted. Originally, websites used a protocol called **HTTP (HyperText Transfer Protocol)** to transfer data between your browser and the website. A protocol (like HTTP) is like a language that your browser and web servers use to talk to each other. But here is the problem: HTTP is outdated and insecure because it sends your data as plain, readable text. This means that anyone with the right tools could potentially see or intercept the information you are sharing online, like passwords or credit card details.

That is where **HTTPS (HyperText Transfer Protocol Secure)** comes in. The 'S' stands for 'secure,' and it is a safer version of HTTP. HTTPS still communicates the HTTP language, but it applies to a secure layer on top of HTTP communication, where the data is encrypted for the remainder of the communication exchange between your device and the website. This technique makes it much harder for hackers to intercept or tamper with your information. In simple terms, it keeps your online activity private and secure.

Today, most of the internet web services have moved to HTTPS. In fact, according to Google, around 95% of all web browsing is now done using HTTPS, and on Google Chrome, 99% of browsing time is on HTTPS-protected sites. Plain old HTTP is rejected by most systems today, which is a good practice that you should follow as a user. You will notice this when you visit most websites today. It will show at the beginning of the web address you entered or click on: →**https**://www.google.com/

Here is the difference between HTTP and HTTPS and how they work.

HTTP

With an HTTP conversation, information from the user is requested from your system (PC, Smartphone etc.) in clear text to the Web Service.

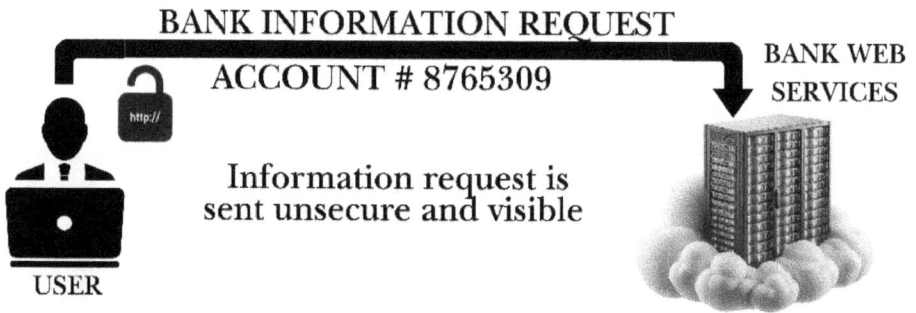

BANK INFORMATION REQUEST

ACCOUNT # 8765309

BANK WEB SERVICES

Information request is sent unsecure and visible

USER

The Web service then returns the requested information to your system in clear text, exposing your information, including any sensitive information with no protection. With HTTP, a hacker could easily read the plain text code and steal your information.

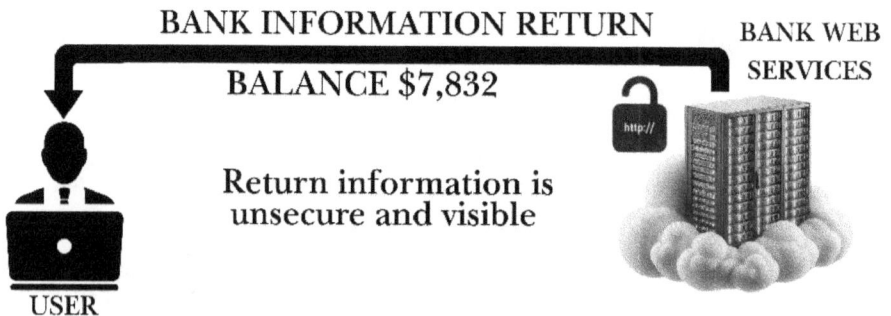

BANK INFORMATION RETURN

BALANCE $7,832

BANK WEB SERVICES

Return information is unsecure and visible

USER

HTTPS

With an HTTPS conversation, the initial request from your system (PC, Smartphone etc.) to the Website includes a request to agree on a secret conversation. This secret conversation is achieved by 1) Validating the website has a certificate acknowledging it been identified as a known and trusted service 2) The two parties in the conversation agree on a key (secret password) to be used throughout the remainder of the conversation.

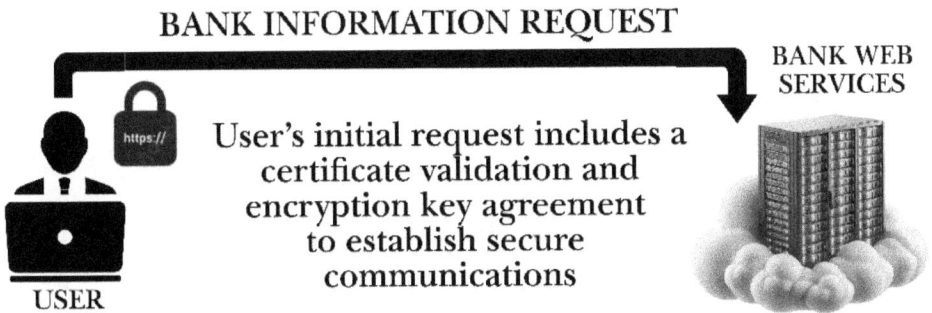

BANK INFORMATION REQUEST

BANK WEB SERVICES

User's initial request includes a certificate validation and encryption key agreement to establish secure communications

USER

This key is a public key (secret passcode) that is then used to establish a secondary layer of private keys, called session keys. These keys are then used to encrypt the data during transport across networks. And then decrypt the data upon arrival for the remainder of the conversation between the two systems, keeping it secret and secure and away from prying eyes.

RETURN BANK INFORMATION

BANK WEB SERVICES

BALANCE IS ENCRYPTED (i.e. - Z2x6CWL2WslImcCQ=)

If secure communications is established, conversation proceeds in ENCRYPTED form and information is protected

USER

However, do not Trust HTTPS Alone

While HTTPS helps protect your data by encrypting the conversation, it is not enough to trust HTTPS or a padlock symbol. Cybercriminals have found ways to circumvent the certificate process and masquerade a website as safe. You should always try to validate the site as a trusted domain or organization before using their services. The following are tips for tools that will help perform those tasks.

DNS Filtering

DNS stands for Domain Name System. DNS is like the internet's phonebook, it translates human-friendly domain names (like www.google.com) into IP addresses (like 142.250.190.14) that computers use to identify each other on the network. So, when you enter a web address in your browser, this address is converted into a number address (like a telephone number) which is unique to every web service. DNS filtering blocks access to malicious, inappropriate, or unwanted websites by intercepting DNS requests and deciding whether to allow or block them based on rules or threat intelligence.

Instead of resolving the domain name to its IP address like usual, it can:
- Allow the request (for safe sites)
- Redirect the user (to a warning page)
- Block request entirely for (malware, phishing, adult content, etc.) sites.

Use a secure DNS service to block access to harmful or inappropriate websites.

How DNS Filtering Is Acquired
There are two main ways to get DNS filtering for individual use:

1. **Use a Public DNS Filtering Provider**
   These are easy to set up, just change your DNS settings.

Provider	Features	Cost
OpenDNS	Family & business filtering, reports	Free & Paid
CleanBrowsing	Blocks adult/malware/phishing content	Free & Paid
Quad9	Blocks known malicious domains	Free
NextDNS	Fully customizable filtering & logs	Free & Paid

No software is needed, just change DNS settings on your router or device. Depending on the device, this may take some help that you can acquire through a simple web search.

2. Install DNS Filtering Software or Agents

If you do not already have Anti-Virus protection or some type of cybersecurity protection software that already includes this service, you can acquire endpoint agents or apps that control DNS requests per device or user. Many of these are used in schools and businesses that may be preinstalled and protecting you already. These are covered in the following topics.

Web Filtering Software

- Install web filtering software to block access based on categories (e.g., gambling, adult content, malware).
- Net Nanny (good for families)

These tools can be configured to align with your specific requirements.

Anti-Virus and Endpoint Protection with URL Filtering

URL filtering is a process used in cybersecurity to control access to websites based on the URLs (Uniform Resource Locators) that users attempt to visit, such as www.websitename.com.

How it Works:

URL filtering involves analyzing the web address (URL) that a user is trying to access and comparing it to a database of categorized URLs. Depending on the web address, the filter will either allow, block, or log the attempt. Use Anti-Virus Software that includes URL filtering capabilities to block specific websites or categories. URLs are also sorted into categories like "social media," "gambling," "adult content," etc., and access can be controlled by category. These categories are known by cybersecurity as Blacklisting and whitelisting. Specific URLs can be blocked (blacklist) or explicitly allowed (whitelist). Some advanced systems scan websites in real time for malicious content or inappropriate material. Some of the better-known home antivirus solutions that include robust web filtering capabilities are Bitdefender Antivirus, AURA, Trend Micro Antivirus, Norton 360, ESET NOD32, and McAfee Antivirus.

Enable Ad Blockers and Anti-Tracking Tools

Use Browser Extensions: Tools like **uBlock Origin, Ghostery, Adblock, Privacy Badge or AdLock**, to block ads and prevent tracking. Real ads from legitimate companies can be annoying on their own, but many online advertisements can be downright dangerous. For example, you may have encountered malicious scareware ads that look like antivirus alerts. Other ads impersonate law enforcement and demand hefty fines. You also want advertisers to know less about you. Ad blockers not only drastically reduce the number of ads you see online, but they also prevent advertisers from tracking your online activities and doing harm. Turning on an ad blocker depends on the device and browser you are using. Here are some popular free options:

- uBlock Origin (Highly recommended)
- Adblock Plus
- AdGuard

Here is a detailed step-by-step guide to install the recommended option uBlock Origin, on the most popular browsers as an example:

DESKTOP BROWSERS
Google Chrome
1. Open Chrome.
2. Go to the Chrome Web Store: Install uBlock Origin for Chrome
3. Click the "Add to Chrome" button.
4. A pop-up will appear. Click "Add extension."
5. Once added, you will see a shield icon in the top-right corner of Chrome.
6. Click the icon to access settings or disable it on certain sites.

Mozilla Firefox
1. Open Firefox.
2. Go to the Firefox Add-ons site: Install uBlock Origin for Firefox
3. Click "Add to Firefox."
4. Confirm by clicking "Add."
5. You will see the uBlock Origin icon in your toolbar.
6. Click it to view stats or manage blocking.

Microsoft Edge
1. Open Microsoft Edge.
2. Go to the Edge Add-ons store: Install uBlock Origin for Edge
3. Click "Get", then confirm with "Add extension."
4. Once installed, it will appear in the toolbar.
5. Click it to manage or turn it off for certain pages.

Safari (macOS)
Safari does not support uBlock Origin, but you can use AdGuard or 1Blocker. Using AdGuard:
1. Open the App Store on your Mac.
2. Search for AdGuard for Safari.
3. Install the app.
4. Open System Preferences > Extensions or Safari > Settings > Extensions and enable AdGuard.
5. In Safari > Preferences > Websites > Content Blockers, ensure AdGuard is enabled for all websites.

MOBILE DEVICES

iPhone / iPad (Safari)

1. Open the App Store.
2. Search and download either:
   - AdGuard
   - 1Blocker
3. Open the app and follow the setup instructions.
4. Go to Settings > Safari > Extensions and toggle the blocker ON.
5. Also go to Settings > Safari > Content Blockers and enable the installed blocker.

Android

1. **Option 1:** Download the Brave Browser from the Google Play Store and use it instead of Chrome, it is easiest, and it has built-in ad blocking.

Option 2: Use Firefox + uBlock Origin.

1. Install Firefox from the Google Play Store.
2. Open Firefox and go to about:addons.
3. Search for uBlock Origin and install it.

- **Be Wary of Malvertising:** Malicious ads can redirect you to dangerous websites or try to download malware.
- **Disable Third-Party Cookies:** This limits advertisers and trackers from following your online behavior.

Virtual Private Network (VPN)

A VPN, or Virtual Private Network, establishes a secure, private connection between your computer and a remote point on the internet. It creates a point-to-point tunnel that encrypts your communications and personal data, protecting you from prying eyes.

The following diagram summarizes how a VPN service works:

Imagine the internet as a vast network with millions of connections and communications flowing across it worldwide. Normally, your data travels through this network alongside everyone else's, making it more vulnerable to interception.

A VPN, however, builds a private, encrypted connection between you and the web services you want to access. This ensures that only you and your intended recipients can see and understand the data being exchanged.

Think of it like being in a crowded room where everyone is speaking the same language, anyone nearby can hear and understand the conversations. Now imagine that you and a friend switch to speaking in a language only the two of you understand. Even though others can hear you talking, they cannot comprehend what you are saying. That is the privacy a VPN provides.

- **Use VPNs on Public Wi-Fi:** When connected to open networks (e.g., cafes, airports), a VPN ensures that your browsing activity is secure.
- **Choose Reputable VPN Providers:** Avoid free VPN services, which may collect and sell your data. A trusted group of services to choose from are: ExpressVPN, NordVPN, Surfshark, CyberGhost, Private Internet Access (PIA). Some cybersecurity protection software like Anti-Virus applications have VPN services included as well.

Avoid Public Wi-Fi for Transactions of Sensitive Information

- **Disable Automatic Wi-Fi Connections:** This prevents your device from connecting to unknown networks.
- **Use Mobile Data (Cellular Service) for Financial Transactions:** Public Wi-Fi is more vulnerable to hacking attempts, making it risky for banking or personal data exchanges.
- **Turn Off File Sharing:** When on public networks, disable file sharing reduces the chance of unauthorized access.

Download Only from Trusted Sources

- **Use Official App Stores:** Install apps from legitimate platforms such as Google Play, Apple's App Store, or software vendor websites.
- **Warning!** If you find your experiencing issues with software, be cautious before clicking on anything initiating support. Contact the source company for support to be safe.
- **Avoid Pirated Software:** These can have hidden malware or spyware.
- **Check File Extensions:** Be wary of unexpected file types (like .exe, .bat, or .vbs) that could execute malicious code.

Keep Your Software and Systems Updated

- **Update Operating Systems and Apps:** Security vulnerabilities are regularly discovered and patched in updates. This is one of the biggest concerns of cybersecurity professionals. The more systems are up to date across the internet, the lower the risk.
- **Enable Automatic Updates:** One of the simplest yet most effective ways to protect yourself from cyber threats is to keep your software up to date. The best way to stay on top of security updates is to let your devices do it for you automatically. Enabling automatic software updates ensures that your operating system, apps, and even your antivirus software stay current without you having to lift a finger. This is crucial because, once a vulnerability is discovered, attackers move quickly to exploit it. If your system is outdated, it is like leaving the front door of your house unlocked.
- **Validate your updates and backups are being performed:** The frequency of you performing this task establishes the currency of your protection.

Here is a quick guide to turning on automatic updates for the most popular home systems:

- **Windows:** Go to **Settings > Update & Security > Windows Update,** then click Advanced options to turn on automatic updates.
- **macOS:** Open **System Preferences > Software Update** and check **Automatically keep my Mac up to date.**
- **iOS & Android**: Navigate to **Settings > General > Software Update** on iOS or **Settings > Software Update** on Android, then toggle on **Automatic Updates**.
- Your various home devices like Smart TV's usually have an option as well.

Manage Browser Extensions Wisely

- **Use Trusted Extensions:** Only install extensions from reputable sources, as some may collect or leak your data.
- **Review Permissions:** Be cautious of extensions, asking for extensive permissions (e.g., access to all websites you visit).
- **Disable or Remove Unused Extensions:** Keeping unused extensions installed can expose you to unnecessary risks.

Control Your Digital Footprint and Privacy Settings

- **Review Privacy Settings:** Adjust privacy controls in your browser, social media accounts, and online services.
- **Clear Cookies and Cache Regularly:** This helps prevent tracking and improves security. The following are the instructions at the time of this printing:

Google Chrome
- Open Chrome: Click the **three dots** (⋮) in the top-right corner.
- Go to **Settings > Privacy and security**: Click **"Clear browsing data."**
- In the popup: Set **Time range** to **"All time"** (or pick another).
- Check **"Cached images and files."**
- (Optional) Leave **Browsing history** and **Cookies** unchecked if you

want to keep them.
- Click **"Clear data."**

Mozilla Firefox
- Open Firefox: Click the **three horizontal lines** (≡) in the top-right.
- Go to **Settings** (or **Options**).
- Select **Privacy & Security** from the left panel.
- Scroll to **Cookies and Site Data**.
- Click **"Clear Data..."**
- Check **"Cached Web Content"** only.
- Click **"Clear."**

Microsoft Edge
- Open Edge.
- Click the **three dots** (⋮) in the top-right.
- Go to **Settings** > **Privacy, search, and services**.
- Under **Clear browsing data**, click **"Choose what to clear."**
- Set the **Time range** to **All time.**
- Check **"Cached images and files"**.
- Click **"Clear now."**

Safari (Mac)
- Open Safari: Click **Safari** in the top-left menu bar, then choose **Preferences**.
- Go to the **Advanced** tab.
- Check **"Show Develop menu in menu bar."**
- Now go to the top menu bar and click **Develop > Empty Caches**.
- You can also clear history and cache by going to:
  Safari > Clear History → choose a time range → click **Clear History.**

MOBILE DEVICES
Chrome on Android/iOS
- o Open Chrome: Tap the **three dots** (⋮) > **History.**
- o Tap **Clear browsing data.**

- o Set the **Time range** to **All time**.
- o Check **"Cached images and files"**.
- o Tap **Clear data**.

Safari on iPhone/iPad
- o Open **Settings**: Scroll down and tap **Safari**.
- o Tap **"Clear History and Website Data."**
- o Confirm when prompted.

Firefox on Mobile
- o Open Firefox.
- o Tap the **three dots** > **Settings**.
- o Tap **Delete browsing data**.
- o Check **Cache**, then tap **Delete browsing data**.

Limit the Personal Information You Share Online: Avoid oversharing on social media, as attackers may use this information for social engineering attacks.

Monitor Accounts and Use Alerts

- **Set Up Account Alerts:** Many services (e.g., banking apps, email) offer notifications for suspicious activities like excessive withdrawals and account changes.
- **Monitor Your Online Accounts:** Regularly check for unauthorized transactions or changes in account details.

Beware of Browser Autofill Risks

- **Disable Autofill for Sensitive Data:** Autofill can be exploited by malicious websites or forms.
- **Use Password Managers Instead:** Password managers are safer and more secure than browser autofill features.

Log Out from Shared Devices

- **Always Log Out of Accounts:** When using shared or public devices, like a hotel desktop, ensure you log out after use. Do not just close the windows or browser. You should click on logout itself.

- **Use Private Browsing Modes:** Private or incognito modes ensure no browsing history or cookies are saved on shared devices.

Educate Yourself on the Latest Threats

- **Stay Informed About Emerging Threats:** Read security blogs and follow reliable cybersecurity news sources. Following are few reliable sources:
  - The Hacker News
  - CSO Online
  - Infosecurity Magazine
  - Security Weekly
  - Cybercrime Wire
  - DarkReading
  - Krebs on Security
  - Cyble Blog
  - Security Ledger
- **Teach Others Safe Browsing Practices:** Educate family members or colleagues about common scams and safe browsing behaviors.

Conclusion

Safe internet browsing practices are essential to protect your personal data, avoid malware, and prevent falling victim to cyberattacks. By following these guidelines, such as using secure browsers, avoiding phishing links, and employing VPNs, you can significantly reduce your online risks. Staying informed and cautious ensures a safer, more enjoyable internet experience. Using HTTPS websites is one of the most basic yet essential internet safety practices. It ensures that data stays encrypted and protected from attackers, builds trust with users, and enhances the overall security of your online experience. However, always validate your domains!

Chapter 7

Securing Home Networks and Wi-Fi

🔑

Securing Home Networks and Wi-Fi

Securing your home network and Wi-Fi is essential to protect your personal devices and data from unauthorized access and cyberattacks. With a secure setup, you can prevent intrusions, protect your devices from malware, and keep sensitive information safe. I understand, some of these tasks can be a little ambitious for home users, but with the following information and a little effort, the key components for securing your technology can be achieved. And if you are up to it, you can try the more advanced tasks. These additional steps will go a long way in providing an elevated level of protection. Following is comprehensive guidance for the best practices in securing your home networks.

Change Your Internet Router's Default Settings

Your Internet Router is typically the last piece of equipment between your home networks and the Internet. It is what connects your home networks to the Internet. There will be a connection to your Internet Service Provider (Usually a cable, sometimes Wireless), and a connection to your home networks (Usually a cable, sometimes Wireless). Sometimes your Wi-Fi services are included in this piece of equipment, so you may just have one device. And in some deployments, you may have separate pieces of equipment for network expansion throughout your home. Especially, where larger Wi-Fi coverage areas are needed. Changing the default settings on these devices is one of the most important steps to prevent unauthorized access. If your equipment is provided by your Internet Service Provider, they should have already done this for you. If you are not sure, just ask yourself, "Who installed the equipment? Who owns the equipment? They should know the password. What is the Wi-Fi System default Username and Password? Like most systems, a router or Wi-Fi system (sometimes both and the same device) have a default username and password, which are credentials used to access the system controls and settings. These default access credentials are meant to get a person who will be managing the system from this point forward access until they can establish better and personal credentials. These credentials have top level privileges and control everything related to your internet access, Wi-Fi services in some cases. This system also controls whom and what have access to your home networks and every device on them. If you need assistance, there are usually videos on YouTube helping with these setups, even for your device. See Diagram Below for help identifying the devices:

Diagram of Meeting Point Between Your Home Networks and Your Service Provider

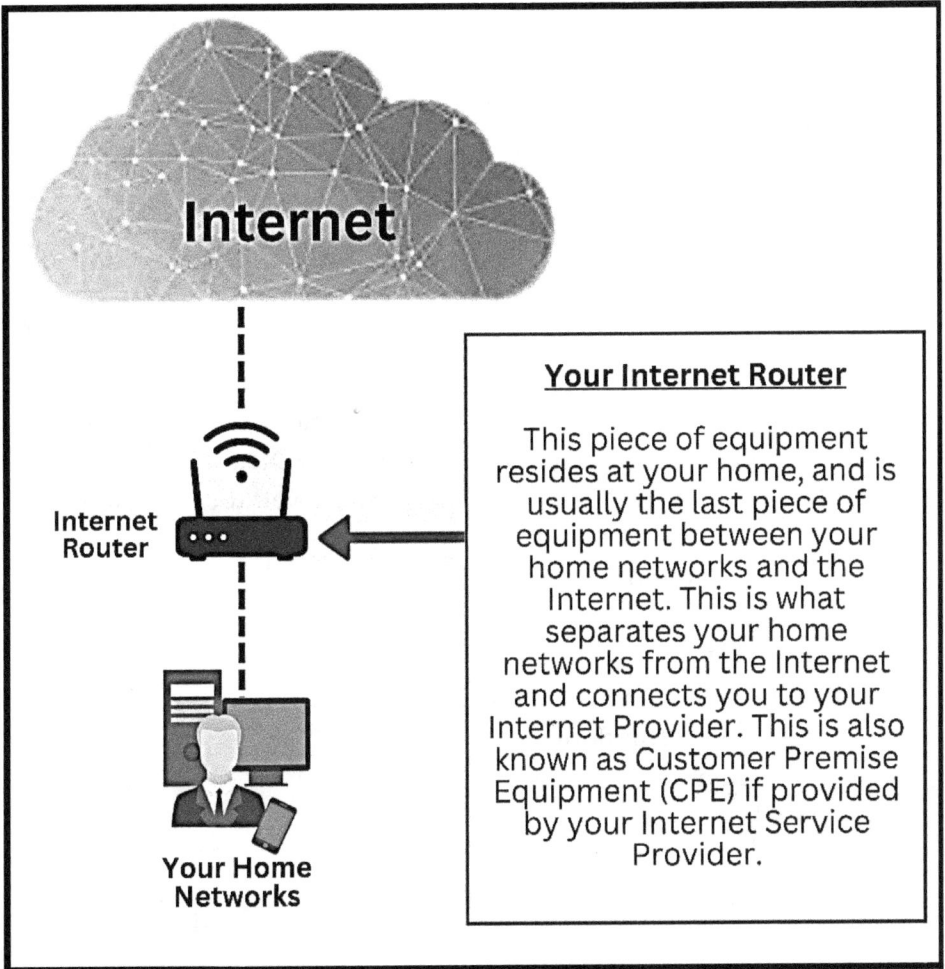

- **Use Strong, Unique Credentials:** Default usernames and passwords are often publicly available, making it easy for hackers to access your router's settings, and your home network and systems.
- **Avoid Predictable Usernames:** Generic usernames like "admin" or "user" are common on routers. Customize the username to make it harder to guess.

Change the Default Wi-Fi Network Name (SSID)
A SSID (Service Set Identifier) is a name for your wireless networks, and an identifier so you can distinguish your wireless networks from others that may be

transmitted into your home or area. These are the network names you see show up when you are connecting to a Wi-Fi network. Your SSID (Wi-Fi network name) might seem harmless, but it can affect your privacy and security. Here are the best practices and recommended SSID types to help keep your network secure and low-profile.

- **Avoid Using Personal Info**
  Do not use your name, address, or anything that identifies you or your home networks (e.g., SmithFamilyWiFi, 123MainSt).
- **Do not Use Default Names**
  Routers often come with default SSIDs that reveal the manufacturer, making it easier for hackers to find and exploit vulnerabilities specific to that model of equipment. Default names like Netgear123, Linksys, or ATT-WiFi can expose what make of router you use, making targeted attacks easier. In some cases, it is extremely easy.
- **Make It Boring or Generic**
  Use something uninteresting to avoid attention from hackers or neighbors.
  Recommended SSID Types
  Generic + Random
    - HomeNetwork_728
    - WiFi_0413
    - LAN_01A3
    - DeviceNet_49

Enable Encryption

Wi-Fi encryption prevents unauthorized users from connecting to your network and accessing data transmitted over it.

- **Use WPA3 if Available,** WPA3 is the latest Wi-Fi encryption standard, offering robust security against brute-force attacks. Turn this feature On if available. If your router does not support WPA3, use WPA2 as the next best option. If your router does not have these, it may be time for an upgrade.
- **Turn off WPS**: WPS makes connecting to Wi-Fi easier but is known to have serious security weaknesses. Disable it to reduce the attack surface and use WPA3 exclusively instead. WPA3 offers a secure method for

connecting devices without the need for WPS.

- **Avoid WEP and WPA:** These are older encryption tools that are vulnerable to attacks.

Set a Strong Wi-Fi Password

This is a password separate from your device's password. There should be a separate password set for each Wi-Fi network (SSID). More on this below.

- **Choose a Complex Password:** The Wi-Fi password should combine numbers, letters, and symbols.
- **Avoid Common Passwords or Phrases:** Passwords like "12345678" or "password123" make your network vulnerable.

Regularly Update Your Wi-Fi Password

- **Change the Password Periodically:** This prevents unauthorized users from staying connected indefinitely. Does not have to happen every day, but the shorter the window, the better. Note, when you perform this task, all devices using this Wi-Fi network will have to have their passwords updated too.
- **Revoke Access to Unknown Devices:** Changing your Wi-Fi password will disconnect unauthorized people and devices, allowing only trusted users that know the new password back on the network.

Set Up Separate Wi-Fi Networks to reduce Risks

Most routers support multiple networks. Allowing guests on your primary network can increase security risks. Separating networks helps reduce risks. Example: Good practice is to set up a SSID (Wi-Fi network) for your devices around the (Smart TV etc.), a separate network for your mobile devices (tablets, mobile phones), and a separate guest network for extended family or friends that visit. Each of these networks separate the various levels of risk by device type and isolating their activity which helps keeps your main devices secure. With some newer routers, you can also limit the duration and amount of access for networks like your guest network which could impact your important systems.

- **Restrict Access to Local Devices:** Many routers offer options to restrict guest network access to your primary shared devices like printers, and smart TVs for video casting. This is good practice.

Use a Different SSID and Password

- **Use a Unique SSID:** Create a distinct name for your guest network that does not match your primary network.
- **Set a Simple but Secure Password:** Use a different password from your main network and change it periodically if you have many guests. "Guest Network" is fine. Just remember to protect the password, or anyone in the neighborhood (or parked in the neighborhood) can use it and is on your network. And yes, this does happen. In fact, there are websites that list addresses for free access.

Regularly Update Your Router's Firmware

Router firmware updates contain security patches and enhancements that improve the security and performance of your device.

Enable Automatic Updates if Available.

- **Automatic Updates Ensure Timely Security Fixes:** Many modern routers support automatic updates. Enabling this option helps ensure your router has the latest protection against vulnerabilities.

Manually Check for Updates

- **Periodically Check the Manufacturer's Website:** Some routers do not automatically update, so you may need to visit the router settings or the manufacturer's website periodically for updates.
- **Install Updates Promptly:** Update as soon as new firmware is available to protect against newly discovered vulnerabilities.

Disable Remote Management

Remote management allows access to your router settings and potentially your internal systems from anywhere in the world, which increases security risks.

- **Disable if You are Not an Advance User:** Most users do not need remote management enabled, as it can expose your router to external threats.
- **Access Settings Locally:** Access your router settings directly from your home network instead of enabling remote access.
- **Use Strong Authentication and Encryption:** If you must enable

remote management, ensure that it is protected with strong credentials and, if possible, limited to specific IP addresses. This is usually saying your work network IP address range, or the IP address of your mobile device, so that no one else easily has access.

Use Parental Controls (If needed)

Parental controls can add an extra layer of protection by controlling access to certain types of content and setting usage limits.

a. Block Unsafe Websites and Content

- **Restrict Access to Known Malicious Sites:** Many routers allow you to filter or block sites by category (e.g., adult content, gambling).
- **Limit Access to IoT and Personal Devices:** Parental controls can restrict network access for specific devices, reducing the risk of unauthorized usage.

Conclusion

Securing your home network and Wi-Fi involves multiple steps, from changing default settings and enabling strong encryption to monitoring connected devices and updating firmware. These measures help protect your devices and personal data from unauthorized access, malware, and network intrusions. By taking these precautions and regularly reviewing your network security, you can maintain a safe and reliable home network environment.

Chapter 8

Antivirus, Firewalls, and Software

Essential Elements of a Secure Digital Environment

Protecting your devices from cyber threats requires a layered approach. Antivirus software, firewalls, and regular software updates each play a crucial role in keeping your systems secure from malware, hackers, and other threats. Let us explore each element in detail, with best practices for a robust defense strategy.

Antivirus Software: Detect and Remove Malicious Threats

Antivirus programs are designed to detect, block, and remove malicious software (malware) from your devices. This includes viruses, worms, spyware, ransomware, and other harmful applications that can steal data, corrupt files, or compromise system performance.

Selecting a Reliable Antivirus Program

Choose a Trusted Brand: When selecting antivirus and identity protection software, it is important to choose a trusted and reputable brand. Established products to consider include:

- **Windows Defender** (built into Windows 10 and 11)
- **Aura**
- **Bitdefender Total Security**
- **Norton 360 with LifeLock**
- **McAfee Total Protection**
- **ESET Smart Security Premium**
- **Trend Micro Maximum Security**
- **Kaspersky** is another widely known option; however, it is considered a higher risk by U.S. government agencies, including the FBI, due to its Russian origins and concerns about national security and potential access to user data by the Russian government. Russia is also known as one of the leading global sources of cybercrime.
- If you are wondering which antivirus is the "best," the answer often comes down to personal preference, just like with any software. A better question might be: **Which one is best for you?** The effectiveness of these tools changes over time as features are updated and threats evolve, so the best choice depends on your needs, technical comfort level, and how much involvement you want in managing your protection.
- Below is a list of key protection features that provide the strongest defense. Getting full coverage at the highest level may require multiple tools. However, if you are not highly technical or want a simplified solution that covers the essential areas with minimal effort, products like **Aura** or **Norton 360** can provide strong, all-in-one protection through a single application.

1. Real-Time Threat Protection

- Constantly monitors files, downloads, and app behavior for suspicious activity.
- Uses AI/machine learning to detect new and unknown threats (zero-day attacks).

2. Web Protection / URL Filtering
- Blocks malicious or phishing websites before you even load them.
- Often integrates with browser extensions to prevent dangerous clicks.

3. Behavior-Based Detection (Heuristics)
- Detects malware by analyzing how files act, not just based on known signatures.
- Useful for catching ransomware or stealthy Threats.

4. Ransomware Protection
- Prevents unauthorized encryption of files.
- Includes safe folders or rollback features to recover unencrypted copies.

5. Firewall Management
- Adds a smart firewall to monitor incoming/outgoing network traffic.
- Alerts you to suspicious or unauthorized communication attempts.

6. Vulnerability Scanner
- Scans for outdated software, unpatched OS files, weak passwords, and open ports.
- Suggests or automate updates.

7. Secure VPN (Virtual Private Network)
- Encrypts your internet connection, especially on public Wi-Fi.
- Prevents tracking and IP/location exposure.

8. Password Manager
- Stores and autofill's passwords securely.
- Often includes password strength checks and breach monitoring.

9. Multi-Device Protection

- Protects not just PCs, but also Macs, Android, and iOS devices under one subscription.
- Includes device tracking and remote wipe for mobile.

10. Identity Theft Protection
- Monitors dark web for stolen credentials, SSNs, credit card numbers.
- Alerts if your info has been compromised.

11. System Optimizer Tools
- Cleans junk files, manages startup programs, and improves performance.
- Helpful for older systems.

12. Parental Controls
- Blocks inappropriate content.
- Tracks screen time and app usage by kids.

13. Sandbox or Application Control
- Runs suspicious files in an isolated environment before allowing them on your system.
- Prevents malware from affecting your main OS.

14. Webcam and Microphone Protection
- Alerts you when apps try to access your camera or mic.
- Allows blocking all access except for trusted apps.

15. Encrypted File Vault / File Shredder
- **Vault:** Stores sensitive files in a password-protected, encrypted area.
- **Shredder:** Securely deletes files so they cannot be recovered.

Consider Features Beyond Basic Protection: Modern antivirus solutions often include great tools. You should also consider advanced features like the following:

1. Credit Monitoring
Tracks your credit file for changes that may indicate fraud or identity theft.

What It Watches:
- New credit inquiries
- New account openings (credit cards, loans)
- Address changes
- Missed payments.
- Credit limit increases or decreases.

Credit Bureau Coverage:
- **Single-bureau monitoring**: Usually from **Experian**.
- **Three-bureau monitoring**: Covers **Experian, Equifax, and TransUnion**, more thoroughly.
  Example Services:
- Aura, Norton LifeLock, IdentityGuard, Credit Karma (free, limited)

2. Mortgage Monitoring

Monitors public and personal data sources for unauthorized activity related to **your home or mortgage**.

What Can It Detect:
- Fraudulent attempts to **refinance** or **transfer ownership** of your home.
- **Home title theft**, where someone tries to file paperwork to "steal" your property.
- **New liens**, changes in ownership records, or suspicious activity at the county level.

Where It Looks:
- County recorder's offices
- Title databases
- Public land records

Often Called:
- **Home Title Monitoring**
- **Property Monitoring**

Note: Some services include **Title Insurance** for coverage (e.g., up to $1 million) if someone fraudulently tries to claim your property.

3. Bank Account & Transaction Monitoring

Keeps an eye on linked financial accounts in real-time.

Alerts You To:
- Unusual purchases or withdrawals

- New accounts opened in your name.
- Changes in account balances
- Suspicious login activity

4. Dark Web Monitoring

Scans the dark web for leaked or stolen personal and financial data.

Watches For:
- Social Security Numbers (SSN)
- Credit card numbers.
- Mortgage account numbers.
- Email and passwords.

5. Identity Verification Monitoring

Alert you if your identity is being used to:
- Apply for a **loan or mortgage.**
- Access government benefits
- Register a **business or domain** in your name.

6. SSN Trace & Monitoring

Monitors your Social Security Number for:
- New aliases, names, or addresses linked to your SSN.
- Activity involving minors' SSNs (child identity protection)

7. Credit Score Tracker

Let you see your credit score regularly and monitor changes.
- Sometimes updated monthly or in real time.
- Includes tips to **improve your credit health.**

Configuring Antivirus for Maximum Protection

- **Enable Real-Time Scanning:** This feature continuously scans files and internet traffic as you use them, blocking threats before they can infect your device.
- **Schedule Regular Full System Scans:** While real-time protection catches many threats, a full system scan can identify dormant or hidden

malware. Weekly or biweekly scans are ideal for most users.

- **Enable Automatic Updates:** Antivirus programs often update their virus databases to recognize new threats. Ensure updates are set to install automatically.
- **Run on All Devices:** Ensure all your devices are protected by installing antivirus software on each one, including mobile devices, as they can be vulnerable to mobile-specific threats.

Avoiding Common Pitfalls

- **Do not Ignore Alerts:** If your antivirus flags a file or website as unsafe, do not bypass the warning.
- **Avoid Running Multiple Antivirus Programs Simultaneously:** Running more than one antivirus can cause conflicts and slow down your system. Choose a reliable program and stick with it.

Firewalls: The First Line of Defense in Security

Firewalls can function as barriers between your devices, networks and external threats by monitoring and controlling data based on their level of safety. This can be done on incoming and outgoing traffic. A firewall helps to prevent unauthorized access to your network, protecting your data and devices from hackers and malware. The general practice by default is to only permit data requests from trusted systems that are on your home network (Inside the Firewall), and block anything that is untrusted or on the Internet (Outside the firewall). So, in simple terms, all requests should be submitted by a trusted person/system you trust from inside your home. Anything on the outside should be deemed dangerous unless you know otherwise. Think of your home network as your digital castle, and the internet beyond as a wild landscape, fascinating and empowering, but only safe if you travel wisely and defend your gates. Although in some instances Internet connectivity can get far more complex, following is a diagram of a typical home Internet Service and a breakdown of its components.

Disable Unused Features

Many routers come with added features that, if left enabled, can be exploited by attackers.

Diagram of Separation Between the Safety of Your Home Networks and the Wild Frontier of the Internet

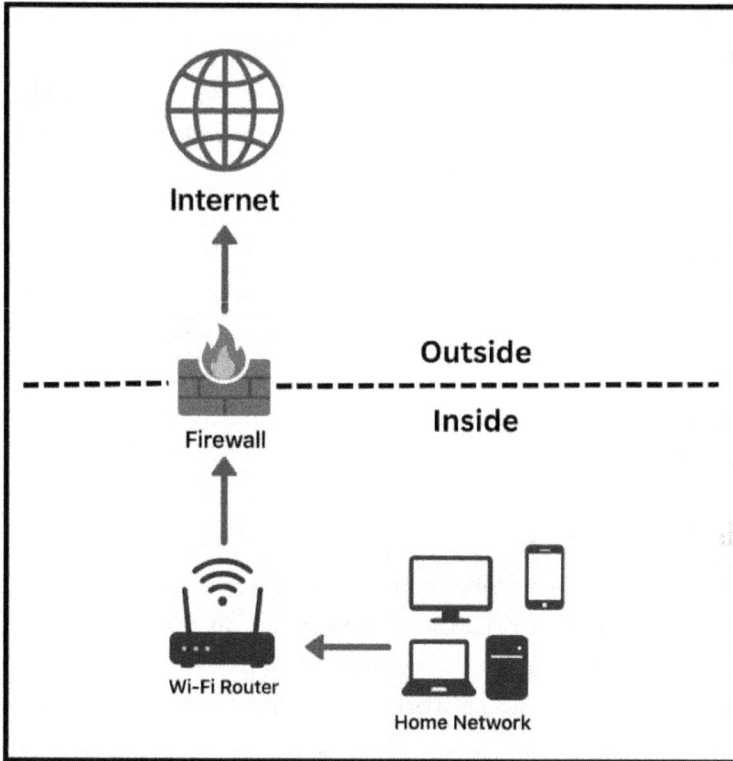

The item labeled Internet represents the Internet outside of your home. This begins with your internet service and extends out to the millions of external networks and systems connected around the world. The item labeled firewall is not unlike the door of your home protecting you from all the external dangers. The Internet encompasses everything outside the door or safety of your home, where everything you are connected to is no longer governed by the rules of your firewall. Imagine the internet outside your home as a vast, unregulated frontier, an endless digital wilderness. The moment data leaves your front door; it enters a world teeming with both opportunity and danger. Just as a dense forest might harbor both beautiful wildlife and hidden predators, the external internet is filled with helpful resources and malicious threats alike. This border firewall is your first line of defense and helps protect you from these harms that could enter. This device is considered a hardware firewall. Border firewalls used to almost always be a totally separate device, but now days they are typically included in the device you have connecting your home network to the Internet. It depends on the Internet Service Provider (ISP) you are receiving your Internet Service from. You could have one, several or in some instances no firewall at all, but you need to make sure you have one. Here are the typical forms of border firewall:

1. Modem/Router Combo provided by your Internet Service Provider (ISP):

- Many ISPs provide a **modem-router combo** device, which often includes **basic firewall functionality.** (such as NAT – Network Address Translation and SPI – Stateful Packet Inspection).
- This is usually sufficient for average households, but it is limited in customization and advanced protections.

2. Homeowner-Provided Router or Firewall:

- Many home users today, especially tech-savvy users or those seeking stronger security often purchase and configure their **own router or dedicated firewall device.** These often are your router for connecting you to the internet, your home firewall and your Wi-Fi router All-in-One.
- These devices (like Ubiquiti, ASUS, and Netgear) offer **enhanced firewall controls,** traffic monitoring, intrusion detection, and more.

3. Dedicated Hardware Firewalls (Less Common):

- Rare in typical homes, but used in higher-risk environments (e.g., small businesses or home offices).
- Devices like **Firewalla, Fortinet, or Ubiquiti UniFi Security Gateway** provide robust perimeter defense.

There are other forms of firewalls which are described below.

Types of Firewalls

- **Software Firewalls:** These firewalls are typically included with most operating systems (such as Windows or macOS) and provide an added layer of protection for individual devices. Software firewalls are easy to configure and provide basic protection for personal users.
- **Hardware Firewalls:** Hardware firewalls are physical devices, often

built into routers, which protect an entire network from external threats. They are beneficial for small offices and homes with multiple connected devices.

- **Cloud-Based Firewalls (Firewall as a Service, or FWaaS):** For more advanced users or businesses, cloud-based firewalls offer flexible, scalable protection for remote and distributed networks. Distributed Networks are environments where a customer has several services operating out of several locations for instance, and they want protection between these services. You would see these firewalls with customers using cloud services that operate in multiple locations where they want added computing power by operating several servers in multiple locations, or redundancy to provide extra stability.

Enable Network Firewalls and Intrusion Detection (If available)

Firewalls and intrusion detection systems (IDS) are powerful tools that add extra layers of protection to your home network. While most home routers come with a basic firewall, intrusion detection systems are still somewhat rare in consumer-grade devices. However, if your device offers IDS, or as this feature becomes more common, it is worth enabling.

What do these tools do?

- **Firewalls** act like a barrier between your home network and the internet, blocking unwanted traffic while allowing safe connections.
- **Intrusion Detection Systems (IDS)** Monitor your network for suspicious activity, either taking action to mitigate the intrusion and/or alerting you if anything unusual is detected. As more advanced options become available in the future, keeping an eye on these features can help you stay one step ahead of potential cyber threats.
- **Enable Your System's Built-in Firewall:** Make sure the firewall on your operating system is enabled, especially when connected to public or untrusted networks.
- **Block Unnecessary Ports and Protocols:** Certain ports are commonly exploited by attackers (e.g., ports for remote desktop connections). Disable any ports or services you do not use to minimize risks.
- **Set Up Rules for Inbound and Outbound Traffic:** Configure specific rules to allow or block traffic from certain IP addresses or domains. This

is particularly useful for securing access to sensitive data or applications.

- **Enabling Notifications:** It can be annoying, but if notification features are available, they can be extremely helpful for unusual activities, such as repeated failed login attempts, so you are aware of any suspicious activity.

Software Updates: Patch Vulnerabilities and Improve Security

Keeping your software up to date is crucial, as updates often include patches for security vulnerabilities that could otherwise be exploited by hackers. This applies to operating systems, applications, and firmware on all devices.

Narrowing the window between the time a software company becomes aware of a vulnerability, identifies a solution, and distributes updates to affected systems, and the moment a malicious cybercriminal unleashes a virus, is critical. For instance, if you have automatic software updates activated but your system settings are set to only check for updates once a month, you are at significantly greater risk compared to a system that checks for updates daily, or even in real-time.

This is why cybersecurity software companies work quickly to identify and address issues, frequently releasing updates, often on a weekly or even daily basis, depending on the severity of emerging threats. Critical security patches are prioritized and rolled out as soon as possible, sometimes resulting in multiple updates within a single day to address urgent vulnerabilities.

One of the most significant concerns in the cybersecurity industry is a "zero-day threat." A zero-day threat refers to a vulnerability that is completely unknown to the manufacturer, when an attack has been deployed. This means the vendor has "zero days" to address the issue before attackers exploit systems. Zero-day threats are especially dangerous because no existing defenses are available at the time of exploitation, leaving systems highly vulnerable until a patch is developed and deployed.

Importance of Software Updates for Security

- **Fix Known Security Vulnerabilities:** Many cyberattacks exploit known vulnerabilities in outdated software. Updates close these security holes, reducing the risk of attacks.
- **Enhance Program Functionality and Stability:** Besides security patches, updates can improve program performance, add new features, and fix bugs that could affect the software's stability.
- **Ensure Compatibility with Other Security Tools:** Updated software often includes changes that make it compatible with newer systems and protections.

Setting Up Automatic Updates

- **Enable Automatic Updates for Essential Software:** Most operating systems and applications have an option to install updates automatically. Enable this for your OS, web browsers, and any frequently used programs.
- **Check Device Firmware for Updates:** Routers, smart home devices, and other IoT gadgets also require firmware updates. Many of these devices have a web interface or app where you can check for updates.
- **Configure a Regular Update Schedule for Work or Business Use:** For devices used in work environments, schedule regular update checks to ensure all applications stay secure without interrupting productivity.

Manual Updates and Exceptions

- **Regularly Check for Updates on Non-Automatic Software:** Some software (e.g., certain gaming applications, open-source tools) may not support automatic updates. Set reminders to check for updates periodically.
- **Delay Updates When Necessary (But Not for Long):** Occasionally, an update may cause compatibility issues. It is okay to delay briefly to ensure compatibility with other critical software, but plan to update as soon as possible.

Best Practices for Using Antivirus, Firewalls, and Software Updates Together

Enable Layered Protection for Comprehensive Security:
- **Use Antivirus and Firewalls in Tandem:** Firewalls function as the

initial gatekeepers by controlling traffic, while antivirus programs identify and neutralize threats that make it onto your system.

- **Rely on Software Updates to Complete the Circle:** Regular updates ensure that both antivirus and firewall defenses remain effective against the latest threats.

Monitor and Adjust Settings as Needed:
- **Review Settings Regularly:** Periodically check antivirus, firewall, and update settings to ensure they remain configured for maximum protection.
- **Set Security Alerts and Notifications:** Enable alerts for critical events like detected threats, blocked connections, and required updates.

Consider All Connected Devices:
- **Protect IoT Devices:** Many smart home devices have basic firewalls and receive occasional firmware updates. Enable these features where possible, as IoT devices can be entry points for cyberattacks.

Conclusion

Antivirus software, firewalls, and software updates form the backbone of any robust cybersecurity plan. Antivirus software protects against viruses and malware, firewalls block unauthorized access, and regular software updates patch vulnerabilities, keeping your devices resilient against cyber threats. Following these best practices ensures that you are actively securing your devices and network, reducing the risk of malware, data breaches, and unauthorized access.

Chapter 9

Backing Up Your Data

🔑

Retaining Your Data for Future Use: A Guide to Protecting Your Personal Files

Backing up your data and protecting your personal files is one of the most important steps to safeguard your personal files, photos, documents, and more from accidental deletion, hardware failure, or malware attacks like ransomware. By creating regular backups, you ensure that your information can be quickly recovered, even in a crisis. Here is a detailed guide to help you set up a comprehensive and reliable data backup system at home. In addition to capturing your data by following the 3-2-1 rule below, it is good practice to retain copies of any applications on CD format you have purchased.

Store Backups in Multiple Locations
- **Follow the 3-2-1 Backup Rule:**
    - **3** – Keep **three** copies of your data. A popular option is: Your Primary Storage Copy Used Daily + A Copy on an External Drive + A Cloud Backup Copy
    - **2** – Store those copies on **two distinct types of media**
    - **1** – Keep **one copy offsite** (physically or in the cloud)

Let us say you have 10 years of precious family photos stored on your computer.

1. Primary Copy (Original)
- Stored on your **home computer** (internal hard drive)

2. Secondary Copy (Local Backup)
- Backed up to an **external hard drive** connected to your computer (different media type)

3. Third Copy (Offsite/Cloud Backup)
- Backed up to a **cloud storage service** like Google Drive, Dropbox, Backblaze or iDrive.

Why This Works:
- If your computer fails, you have copies of your files on your external drive.
- If your house is damaged (fire, theft, flood), the cloud backup is still safe.
- Different media types reduce the risk of failure due to technology failure or data format issues.

Types of Backups and Scheduling

Full Backup
- **What It Is:** A complete copy of all your selected files and folders. This backup includes every file and system configuration, making it the most comprehensive option in case you must perform a total rebuild of your

system.
- **Pros:** Quick recovery, as all files are in one place.
- **Cons:** Requires more storage and takes longer to create.
- **When to Perform:** Periodically (e.g., monthly) as a baseline backup, with incremental backups in between.

Incremental Backup
- **What It Is:** Only backs up files that have changed since the last full backup.
- **Pros:** Saves storage space and time by avoiding duplicate copies of unchanged files.
- **Cons:** Restoration may require multiple backups, as it pulls from both full and incremental backups.
- **When to Use:** For daily or weekly backups to keep your data as up to date as possible without taking up excessive storage.

Differential Backup
- **What It Is:** Backs up files that have changed since the last full backup (different from incremental, which backs up since the last backup of any type).
- **Pros:** Easier to restore than incremental, as it needs only the last full and the last differential backup.
- **Cons:** Can consume up more space over time, as it stores all changes since the last full backup.
- **When to Use:** For a middle-ground approach to storage and ease of recovery.

Mirror Backup
- **What It Is:** A real-time backup that mirrors your files as you save or change them.
- **Pros:** Always ensures an exact replica of your files.
- **Cons:** Can also replicate unwanted changes or deletions, so accidental deletions or corrupt files may be mirrored as well.
- **When to Use:** Ideal for high-priority files you need access to immediately but best combined with other backup types.

Backup Locations: Local, External, and Cloud Options

There are three ways to back up your data. These three options are as follows:

Local Backups (Within your computer)

- **Internal Storage:** Creates a backup on your device's internal storage, such as a different partition. However, this option is vulnerable if your device fails.

Local Backups (External to Computer)

1. **External Hard Drives:** Use a dedicated external drive for backups. External drives are dependable, affordable, and easily accessible.
   - **Tip:** Choose a drive with at least double the capacity of your primary storage.
   - **Popular Options:** Western Digital, Seagate, and Samsung offer reliable external drives.

   Best Practice: Store the external drive in a safe place and unplug it from your computer when not in use to avoid risks of malware propagation.

2. **Network Attached Storage (NAS)**
   - **What It Is:** A small, independent server that connects to your home network and stores data from multiple devices around your home.
   - **Pros:** Can access your data from anywhere on your home network, and some options offer cloud access.
   - **Cons:** Initial setup and configuration may be more complex, and it may cost more than a basic external drive.
   - **Best For:** Multi-user households, smart home devices and setups, and users needing regular backups from multiple devices.

Cloud Backups

- **Online Backup Services:** Services like Backblaze, Carbonite, Google Drive, iDrive, Dropbox, iCloud, (Microsoft) OneDrive, and other dedicated backup services offer remote storage that is accessible from anywhere.
- **Pros:** Automatic, more secure, and allows access to data from remote locations.
- **Cons:** Subscription-based and uploading large files may take time depending on internet speed. Also, some cloud backup services do not use encryption, so if you do not use an application to encrypt the data before it leaves your PC, your data may potentially be accessible by at least the vendor. Applications like Cryptomator can manage this function for you.
- **Best For:** Important files and data you need to access frequently or share across devices. Also acts as a fail-safe if local backups are destroyed or inaccessible.

These are excellent options for everyday home users, as they are easy to set up and use. If you are already a Microsoft 365 or Google user, I highly recommend storing your working files in these cloud environments.

Backups of your files are managed automatically by the cloud service. Files can be configured to save in real time, helping protect your data in the event of a power outage or system failure. This makes file recovery and sharing across devices or with others extremely easy, and it also offers robust file versioning. If you ever need to retrieve an older version of a file, recovery typically takes just a few clicks and a matter of seconds.

In terms of collaboration, multiple users can work on the same file simultaneously, eliminating the need to pass files around, reducing the risk of data loss and improving both efficiency and consistency of ideas. It also reduces the duplication of files and storage consumption when files are passed around.

Best Practices for Data Backup Security

Encrypt Your Backups

- **Protect Sensitive Data:** Enable encryption to ensure that only you can access your data, especially when storing backups on external drives or the cloud.
- **Use Built-In Encryption:** Many backup software and cloud services offer encryption options; enable them for added security.

Use Strong Passwords and Two-Factor Authentication (2FA)

- **Cloud Services:** Use unique, strong passwords for cloud backup services and enable 2FA for an extra layer of security.
- **External Drives:** If storing sensitive information, consider encrypting the drive itself with a tool like **BitLocker** (Windows) or **FileVault** (macOS).

Evaluate Your Backups Regularly

- **Verify Backups:** Periodically check your backups to ensure files can be accessed and restored successfully.
- **Practice Restoring Files:** Evaluating the restore process familiarizes you with it and ensures you can recover files quickly in an emergency.

Implementing Backup for Specific File Types

Photos and Videos

- **Set Up Automated Cloud Syncing:** Services like Google Photos, iCloud, and Amazon Photos offer automatic uploads for mobile devices making back-ups of your files as you create them. So, backup copies are performed daily and in most cases in real-time.

Documents and Personal Files

- **Use Cloud Storage for Real-Time Access and Backup:** Storing documents in Google Drive, Dropbox, or OneDrive allows you to work from anywhere and automatically synchronizes updates.
- **Encrypt Important Documents:** If you use an external drive, consider encrypting sensitive files like tax records or personal documents. The top cloud storage providers also offer encryption features.

System Files and Applications

- **Full Disk Backup for OS and Software:** A full backup of your system can save you from reinstalling software and reconfiguring settings after a crash.
- **Bootable Backup Option:** Some backup tools allow you to create bootable backups, useful for quickly restoring your computer to a fully operational state.

Original Application Software 🛡

The above method of capturing your System Files and Applications should be good enough, but if you are concerned about your original CD's, you can create ISO Image Files (Digital Copies) of your original CD's.

1. **Making Digital Copies**
   - Use software like:
     - **ImgBurn** (Windows)
     - **PowerISO**
     - **WinCDEmu**
     - **macOS Disk Utility** (on older Macs)
   - Save as **.ISO or .DMG** (disk image) files.
   - These preserve the **entire structure** of the CD, including any install files, license data, or auto-run functionality.

2. **Label and Organize**
   - Name each ISO with the software title and version: Photoshop_CS3_Install.iso
   - Include a text file (ReadMe.txt) in the same folder with:
     - The **license key or activation code**
     - **Install instructions** (if needed)
     - Date of backup

3. **Store on Multiple Devices (Apply the 3-2-1 Rule)**
   - **Primary location**: Local computer or external hard drive
   - **Secondary**: USB stick or NAS device
   - **Offsite**: Encrypted backup in the cloud (Google Drive, OneDrive, iDrive, etc.)

Encrypt sensitive software ISOs that contain license keys using something like

VeraCrypt or **BitLocker.**

4. Test the Images Periodically

- Mount the ISO files with a virtual drive tool (e.g., **WinCDEmu,** **DAEMON Tools,** or built-in Windows 10+ features)
- Ensure they **are still installed correctly** and are **not corrupted.**

5. Keep Your Original Discs Safe (Optional)

- Store CDs in a **dry, cool location,** away from sunlight.
- Use **plastic sleeves or jewel cases** to prevent scratches.

6. Track License Information Separately

- Use a **password manager** or encrypted file to store:
  - License keys
  - Order confirmation emails.
  - Serial numbers

Conclusion

Backing up your data regularly ensures that you can recover quickly from data loss, whether caused by hardware failure, accidental deletion, or a cyberattack. By combining local and cloud backups, following a consistent backup schedule, and securing your backups with encryption and strong passwords, you can protect your files and ensure they are accessible when needed. Following these best practices for data backup at home provides peace of mind that your important files, photos, and personal information are safe.

PROTECTING YOUR PRIVACY ONLINE

Chapter 10

Social Media Security and Privacy Settings

🔑

As more personal activities and transactions move online, protecting your privacy has become crucial for staying safe in the digital age. Online privacy involves safeguarding personal information from being tracked, collected, and misused by websites, advertisers, cybercriminals, and even governments. Here is comprehensive information for keeping your personal information private while browsing, shopping, and engaging online.

Social Media Security and Privacy Settings for the Home User

Social media platforms are powerful tools for communication and connection but can also be a source of privacy risks. Personal information shared on social media can be exploited for data mining, identity theft, or phishing. By using built-in security and privacy settings and practicing safe social media habits, you can minimize the risk of a breach of your privacy. Here is a comprehensive guide to securing your social media accounts.

General Best Practices for Social Media Security

- **Use Strong, Unique Passwords**
- **Avoid Reusing Passwords Across Platforms:** Use a unique password for each social media account to prevent hackers from accessing multiple accounts if one password is compromised.
- **Use a Password Manager:** Password managers like NordPass, LastPass, RoboForm, Dashlane, 1Password, Keeper, LogMeOnce, Proton Pass, Bitwarden or Bit Defender can generate and store complex passwords, making it easier to use unique passwords without needing to remember each one.

Enable Two-Factor Authentication (2FA)

- **Add an Extra Layer of Security:** Most social media platforms offer 2FA, which requires a second step (such as a code sent to your phone) in addition to your password. This protects your account even if your password is stolen.
- **Use an Authenticator App:** Apps like Google Authenticator or Authy are more secure than SMS-based 2FA, as SIM-swapping attacks can intercept SMS codes.

Watch for Suspicious Links and Messages

- **Be Cautious with Messages from Unknown Sources:** Phishing attempts often come through social media messaging, so avoid clicking on unfamiliar links.
- **Avoid Sharing Sensitive Information:** Even friends' accounts may be

hacked, so do not share personal or financial details over social media.

Privacy Settings on Major Social Media Platforms

Each social media platform offers privacy settings that control who can see your information, contact you, and follow your activities. Adjusting these settings on popular platforms can help keep your information private.

Facebook Privacy Settings
- **Profile and Timeline Privacy**
  - **Limit Who Can See Your Posts:** Under Settings > Privacy, set "Who can see your future posts?" to **Friends** or a **custom audience** rather than **Public**.
  - **Limit Past Posts Visibility:** Choose **Limit Past Posts** to retroactively change old public posts to "Friends" only.
- **Profile Information**
  - **Limit Who Can See Your Personal Info:** Under Settings > Privacy, restrict profile details (like birthdate, email, and phone number) to **Only Me** or **Friends**.
  - **Hide Friends List:** Change "Who can see your friends list?" to **Only Me** or **Friends** to limit strangers from connecting with your network.
- **Tagging and Timeline Review**
  - **Enable Review for Tagged Posts:** In Settings > Profile and Tagging, enable **Review posts you are tagged in** so you can approve or reject tags before they appear on your timeline.
  - **Restrict Tag Suggestions:** Adjust tag settings so that only **Friends** or **Only Me** can see suggestions to tag you in photos.
- **Control Who Can Find You**
  - **Limit Searchability:** Under Settings > Privacy, set "Who can look you up using the email address/phone number you provided?" to **Friends** or **Only Me**.
  - **Disable Search Engine Indexing:** Toggle off Allow search engines outside of Facebook to link to your profile to prevent your

profile from showing up in search engines like Google.

Instagram Privacy Settings
- **Set Your Account to Private**
  - o **Private Account:** Under Settings > Privacy > Account Privacy, toggle on **Private Account** to limit access to only approved followers.
- **Limit Profile Information and Interactions**
  - o **Hide Activity Status:** In Settings > Privacy > Activity Status, toggle **Show Activity Status** to the offsetting so people cannot see when you are online.
  - o **Restrict Story Viewing and Sharing:** Under Privacy > Story, you can hide your story from certain followers and prevent others from sharing your story as direct messages.
  - o **Approve Tagged Photos Manually:** Under Privacy > Tags, turn on **Manually Approve Tags** so photos do not appear on your profile without your approval.
- **Manage Direct Messages and Comments**
  - o **Limit Message Requests:** Go to Settings > Privacy > Messages to control who can message you directly.
  - o **Filter Offensive Comments:** Under Privacy > Comments, turn on **Hide Offensive Comments** and add any additional custom words you want to filter out.

X (Formally Twitter) Privacy Settings
- **Protect Your Tweets**
  - o **Set Tweets to Private:** In Settings > Privacy and Safety > Audience and Tagging, select **Protect Your Tweets** to make your tweets visible only to followers.
- **Control Tagging and Mentions**
  - o Restrict Photo Tagging: Limit tagging permissions to Only People You Follow or Off.

- o **Manage Mentions and Replies:** In Privacy and Safety, manage who can reply to your tweets to avoid harassment or spam.
- **Control Location Sharing**
  - o **Disable Precise Location:** Go to Settings > Privacy and Safety > Location Information, and toggle off **Precise Location** to avoid sharing your location with tweets.
- **Limit Data Sharing with Partners**
  - o **Disable Personalization and Data Sharing:** Under Privacy and Safety > Data Sharing, turn off **Allow additional information sharing with business partners** to prevent Twitter from sharing your information with third parties.

LinkedIn Privacy Settings
- **Control Who Can See Your Profile and Activity**
  - o **Limit Profile Visibility:** In Settings > Visibility, you can manage who can view your profile, connections, and activity.
  - o Prevent Profile Viewing Notifications: Change Profile Viewing Options to Private Mode if you want to browse other profiles anonymously.
- **Adjust Data Sharing and Advertising Preferences**
  - o **Limit Data Sharing:** Under Data Privacy > Data sharing with third parties, turn off options to restrict LinkedIn from sharing your data.
  - o **Personalized Ads:** Manage your ad preferences in **Advertising data** settings to reduce targeted advertising.
- **Control of Public Profile Visibility**
  - o **Limit Public Profile Details:** Under Settings > Visibility > Edit your public profile, adjust which details can be seen by non-connections.

Keep a close eye out when using tools like Dating Sites.
Dating Sites: Spotting and Avoiding Scammers

1. Watch Out for Love Bombing
- Scammers often shower victims with affection quickly to build trust.
- **Red Flag**: "I've never felt this way before," within a few days of chatting.

2. Never Send Money or Gift Cards
- The #1 red flag is any request for money, especially for emergencies, travel, or family problems.
- **Red Flag**: "I need $500 to fly to see you..."

3. Refuse to Move Conversations Off the Platform Too Quickly
- Scammers often push for WhatsApp, email, or text to avoid platform monitoring.
- **Red Flag**: "Let's talk on Telegram instead, it's more private."

4. Beware of "Overseas" or "Out of Town" Profiles
- Many scammers claim to be deployed in the military, engineers on oil rigs, or traveling for work.
- **Red Flag**: Cannot meet in person. Constant excuses.

5. Use Reverse Image Searches
- Check if their profile photo is stolen. Tools: Google Images, Tineye.
- **Red Flag**: The same photo appears on multiple unrelated profiles.

6. Report Suspicious Behavior
- Most platforms have a **Report** or **Block** button. Use it!

Limit Permissions for Third-Party Apps and Extensions
- Many social media accounts are linked to third-party apps, which may access your data or post on your behalf. Review these connections and limit permissions to protect your information.

Review and Remove Unnecessary Apps
- **Check Authorized Apps Regularly:** In the settings of each social media platform, review apps that have access to your account and

remove any that are no longer necessary.
- o **Limit Permissions for Remaining Apps**
- **Adjust Permissions for Accessing Personal Data:** For apps that need access, limit permissions to essential data only, like avoiding permissions for posting on your behalf or accessing contact lists.

Control What Others Can See and Share About You

- Sometimes, other users' actions can affect your privacy, such as tagging you in posts or sharing your information with others. Manage these settings to control what others can see or do with your information.

Limit Who Can Tag You

- **Review Tags Before Approval:** Most platforms allow you to approve posts in which you are tagged before they appear on your profile.
- **Control Tag Suggestions in Photos:** Some platforms offer an option to disable face recognition or tagging suggestions in photos.
  - o **Avoid Sharing Location Data in Posts**
- **Disable Geotagging:** Avoid enabling location tags in posts, which can reveal your whereabouts and routines.
- **Edit Past Posts to Remove Location Data:** If you have shared location-tagged posts in the past, consider removing the location data to protect your privacy.

Be Mindful of Your Digital Footprint

- **Limit Personal Information in Profiles**
- **Share Only What's Necessary:** Avoid sharing sensitive information like your phone number, home address, or detailed work history that could be used for social engineering.
- **Use a Separate Email Address:** Consider using a different email for social media accounts to avoid linking them to your primary email.

Delete Old Posts or Accounts

- **Review and Delete Old Posts:** Periodically review past posts and delete any that reveal too much personal information or are no longer relevant.

- **Deactivate or Delete Inactive Accounts:** If you no longer use an account, consider deactivating or deleting it to reduce your online footprint.

Think Before You Post

- **Consider Long-Term Impact:** Remember that anything you post online may remain available even after deletion. Think about how future employers, family, or others might interpret your posts.
- **Regularly Review Privacy Policies and Settings**
  o Social media platforms update their policies and privacy settings often. To ensure continued privacy, review your settings periodically and keep up with changes.
- **Schedule Regular Privacy Check-Ups**
- **Review Settings Every Few Months:** Most platforms offer a privacy checkup or audit tool to help you quickly review your settings and adjust as needed.
- **Stay Informed of Policy Changes**
- **Read Notifications from Platforms:** Platforms like Facebook or Instagram notify users of privacy policy updates. Read these notifications to stay informed about how your data is used.

Conclusion

Using social media securely requires setting up strong privacy settings, checking app permissions, and being mindful of the information you share. By implementing these best practices and reviewing privacy settings on major platforms, you can significantly reduce the risk of your personal information being misused. Regular reviews and cautious sharing habits ensure that you stay in control of your online presence and protect your privacy in the long term.

Chapter 11

Managing Your Digital Footprint

○

Your digital footprint includes every account, post, and interaction you have made online. Delete old accounts you no longer use and switch to privacy-focused tools such as VPNs and encrypted messaging apps to minimize your exposure.

Managing Your Digital Footprint for the Home User

Your digital footprint is the trail of information you leave behind whenever you engage with the internet, including websites you visit, posts you make, or information you share. Managing your digital footprint helps protect your privacy, secure your personal data, and maintain a positive online reputation. Here is a comprehensive guide for home users on how to actively manage and minimize their digital footprint.

Understanding Types of Digital Footprints
Active Digital Footprint
- **What It Is:** Information you knowingly share, such as social media posts, comments, email subscriptions, or forum participation.
- **Examples:** Posting photos on Instagram, writing a blog, or sharing updates on Facebook.

Passive Digital Footprint
- **What It Is:** Information collected about you without your direct input, often through website tracking or cookies.
- **Examples:** Your browsing history, IP address, device information, and search terms that websites, social media platforms, and search engines collect.

Minimizing Your Digital Footprint with Privacy Tools
Use Privacy-Focused Browsers
- **Browsers Focused on Security:** These browsers are designed to protect your personal data, minimize online tracking, and enhance anonymity while browsing the internet. Unlike traditional browsers that often collect data for advertising or analytics, privacy-focused browsers emphasize user control and security. Here are some of the most popular options:
    - **Brave** – Blocks ads and trackers by default; includes built-in Tor browsing.
    - **Mozilla Firefox (with settings adjusted)** – Highly customizable with strong privacy controls.
    - **Tor Browser** – Routes traffic through the Tor network for maximum anonymity.
    - **DuckDuckGo Browser (mobile)** – Focuses on search and

browsing without tracking.

- o **Google Chrome (Incognito mode)** – Prevents browsing history and cookies from being saved (but does not hide activity from your ISP, employer, or websites) like a true Privacy-Focused Browser.

- **Disable Third-Party Cookies:** Cookies are small pieces of data that websites store in your browser. Where first-party cookies are created by the website you are currently on. They help with things like keeping you logged in or remembering items in your shopping cart. **Third-party** cookies are created by a different domain or website than the one you are visiting. These typically come from ads, social media buttons, or trackers embedded in the site. Example: You visit a clothing website that has a Facebook "Like" button. That button may place a Facebook cookie in your browser. Later, when you visit a news site with a Facebook ad, Facebook can recognize you and tailor the ads to your interest. Third-party cookies allow advertisers and data brokers to collect a history of what sites you visit, what you click on, and how long you stay. They use this to create a detailed profile and serve you targeted ads. You look at a pair of shoes on one site, then see ads for those shoes on other sites. That is third-party cookies enabling "retargeting" ads. Most browsers allow you to block third-party cookies, which advertisers use to track your activity across multiple websites.

- **Private Browsing Mode:** Browsers' private or incognito modes help limit the local storage of browsing history, although your activity may still be visible to your ISP. Here is how to activate Private Browsing Mode in the most common web browsers:
  - o **Google Chrome (Incognito Mode)**
    - Open Chrome.
    - Click the **three dots** (⋮) in the top-right corner.
    - Select **"New Incognito Window."**
    - A dark window will open with the Incognito icon.
    - **Shortcut:**
      Ctrl + Shift + N (Windows)
      Cmd + Shift + N (Mac)

  - o **Mozilla Firefox (Private Window)**

- Open Firefox.
- Click the **three lines** (☰) in the top-right corner.
- Choose **"New Private Window."**
- You will see a purple mask icon.
- **Shortcut:**
  Ctrl + Shift + P (Windows)
  Cmd + Shift + P (Mac)

---

o **Safari (Private Browsing)**
  - Open Safari.
  - Click **File** in the top menu bar.
  - Select **"New Private Window."**
  - The address bar will turn dark.
  - **Shortcut:**
    Cmd + Shift + N (Mac)

---

o **Microsoft Edge (InPrivate Mode)**
  - Open Edge.
  - Click the **three dots** (⋯) in the top-right corner.
  - Select **"New InPrivate Window."**
  - A dark window labeled "InPrivate" will appear.
  - **Shortcut:**
    Ctrl + Shift + N (Windows)

---

o **Brave Browser (Private or Tor)**
  - Open Brave.
  - Click the **three lines** (☰) or **three dots** (⋮).
  - Choose:
  - **"New Private Window"** for standard private browsing.
  - **"New Private Window with Tor"** for anonymous browsing via the Tor network.

Use Ad Blockers and Anti-Tracking Tools
- **Extensions like uBlock Origin, Privacy Badger, and Ghostery:**

These block ads and trackers, making it harder for advertisers to build a profile on you.

- **Use HTTPS Everywhere:** This extension ensures that you connect to websites over HTTPS (a secure, encrypted protocol) whenever possible, protecting your data in transit.

Use a VPN (Virtual Private Network)

- **Encrypt Your Data:** A VPN hides your IP address and encrypts your online traffic, making it difficult for third parties to track your online activity.
- **Choose a Trusted VPN Provider:** Reputable providers like ExpressVPN, NordVPN, or ProtonVPN offer privacy protections, unlike free VPNs that might log and sell your data.

Regularly Review and Manage Social Media Activity
Limit Personal Information Shared on Social Media

- **Avoid Sharing Sensitive Details:** Do not post your full birthdate, address, phone number, or other personal identifiers.
- **Adjust Privacy Settings:** Use privacy settings to restrict who can see your posts, photos, and personal information. On platforms like Facebook, Instagram, and X (Twitter), set your profile to private or limit visibility to friends only.

Audit Past Posts

- **Delete Unnecessary or Outdated Posts:** Regularly review your social media history, deleting posts that no longer reflect you or that contain sensitive information.
- **Limit Location Sharing:** Avoid sharing your location in posts or turn off geotagging to keep your location history private.

Manage Third-Party Apps and Permissions

- **Revoke Access for Unused Apps:** Many social media accounts are linked to third-party apps, which may continue accessing your data. Regularly review and remove permissions for apps you no longer use.

- **Use Single Sign-On (SSO) with Caution:** While SSO (logging in via Facebook or Google) is convenient, it connects multiple accounts. Consider creating separate logins instead for more control over each account.

---

4. Secure Email and Online Accounts
a. Use Unique, Strong Passwords for Each Account
- **Password Managers:** Tools like 1Password, or Bitwarden securely store passwords and make it easy to use unique credentials for each account.
- **Enable Two-Factor Authentication (2FA):** Adding 2FA provides an extra layer of security, even if a password is compromised.

Create Separate Email Accounts for Different Purposes
- **Use Different Emails for Personal, Professional, and Promotional Use:** This minimizes exposure if one account is compromised and keeps sensitive information separate from general internet activity.
- **Consider Disposable Email Addresses:** Use temporary or disposable email addresses when signing up for newsletters, online offers, or free trials.

Limit Email Tracking
- **Block Tracking Pixels:** Many emails contain tracking pixels to monitor when and where you open emails. A tracking pixel is like a tiny invisible spy for the internet. It is a super small image, usually just one pixel in size or one dot on your screen, which gets hidden in emails or on websites. You typically cannot see it, but when you open an email or visit a web page with a tracking pixel, it quietly sends information back to whoever puts it there.
  That information might include:
  - When you opened the email
  - What kind of device you are using
  - Where you are in the world (based on your internet connection location)

o What you clicked on

Companies use tracking pixels to see how people interact with their emails or websites, kind of like digital footprints. Marketers love them because it tells them what is working. But it also means your actions are being watched, even if you do not realize it. See diagram below:

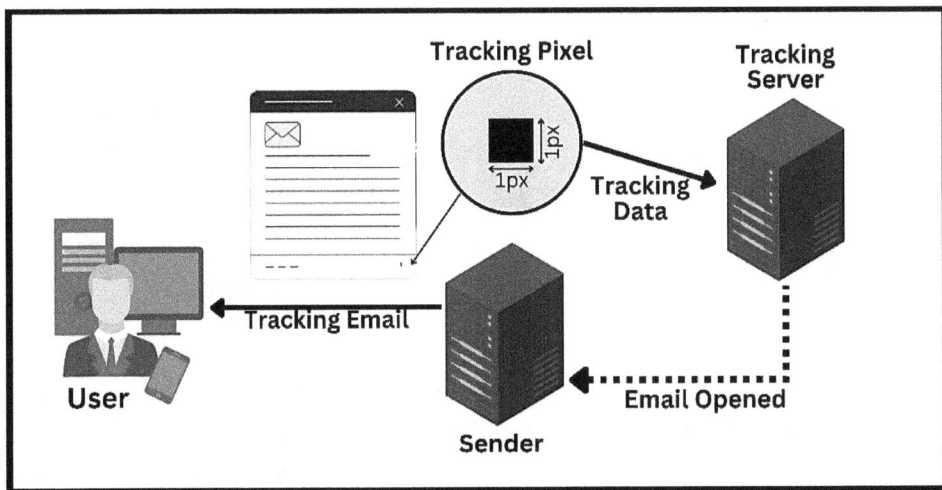

To protect yourself from tracking pixels, especially in emails and websites, here are practical steps anyone can take, even without tech expertise:

o **Use an email extension** - Adding extensions like PixelBlock (Gmail), Trocker (Outlook) and MailTrackerBlocker (Apple Mail on macOS) can block these pixels. Another option is to turn off the automatic loading of images. Most email apps (like Gmail, Outlook, Apple Mail) allow you to turn off automatic image loading.

o For Web Sites protection, using a privacy-focused browser goes a long way to help.

• **Avoid Click-Through Links in Suspicious Emails:** This prevents opening links that might track your IP or lead to phishing websites. A

click-through link is a hyperlink (usually embedded in text, a button, or an image) that takes a user to another webpage or online destination when clicked upon. It is commonly used in emails, ads, websites, and social media to direct users to:

- o Product pages
- o Signup forms
- o Articles or blogs
- o Downloads or exclusive offers

Example of a Click-Through Link:

If an email says:

"Click here to get 20% off your next order."

The words *"Click here"* are the **click-through link**. When you click it, you are sent to a webpage with the discount offer.

Monitor and Manage Search Engine Activity

Use Privacy-Focused Search Engines

- **DuckDuckGo or Startpage:** These search engines do not track your search history or create user profiles, providing more private search results.
- **Adjust Google Privacy Settings:** If you use Google, go to your Google Account > Data & Personalization to review and limit activity tracking and ad personalization.

Regularly Clear Search and Browser History

- **Delete Search History from Accounts:** For Google users, delete or disable **Web & App Activity** to minimize your data footprint.
- **Clear Cache, Cookies, and History in Browser Settings:** This reduces the amount of data stored about you locally and prevents long-term tracking.

Avoid Personalized Search Results

- **Turn Off Ad Personalization:** Platforms like Google and Facebook offer settings to disable personalized ads based on your browsing behavior.

Regularly Delete or Anonymize Old Accounts

Find and Delete Unused Accounts

- **Use Tools like JustDeleteMe or Deseat.me:** These tools help locate accounts linked to your email and guide you on how to delete them.
- **Close Old Accounts:** For accounts you no longer use, consider deleting or deactivating them to reduce data available online.

Use Anonymity When Signing Up for New Accounts

- **Use Pseudonyms or General Usernames:** Avoid using full names or personally identifiable information in usernames and profiles, especially on forums and platforms not tied to personal branding.
- **Separate Registration Emails:** Use an alias or secondary email when signing up for new services to keep your primary email secure.

Manage Your Online Shopping and Financial Footprint

- **Avoid Saving Payment Details:** Many e-commerce sites offer to save your payment details for convenience. Avoid saving them, as data breaches could expose your financial information. Legitimate businesses that process credit cards must follow PCI DSS (Payment Card Industry Data Security Standard) rules. These rules limit how and where card data can be stored. But note I said legitimate businesses. Just like brick-and-mortar stores, be careful to perform your business with reputable companies.

Limit Data Shared with Retailers

- **Only Share Required Information:** Provide only the information necessary for transactions and avoid unnecessary sign-ups if possible.

Monitor and Clean Up Your Digital Footprint Regularly

Google Yourself Periodically

- **Check What's Publicly Available:** Google yourself to see what information is publicly accessible. Address anything sensitive by changing privacy settings, deleting posts, or requesting removal if necessary.
- **Set Up Google Alerts:** Google Alerts let you know whenever an identifier of you (Say your name) appears online, helping you track and manage your online presence. Here is how you set tit up:

Step-by-Step: Set Up Google Alerts for Your Name

1. Go to https://www.google.com/alerts
2. **In the search box**, type your name exactly how you want to monitor it:
   - Use **quotes** for exact matches:
   "John A. Smith" (instead of just John Smith)
3. **Click "Show options"** to customize:
   - **How often:** As-it-happens, once a day, or once a week
   - **Sources:** Blogs, news, web, videos, books, discussions (default is "Automatic")
   - **Language and region:** Customize as needed.
   - **Deliver to:** Your email address or RSS feed.
4. **Click "Create Alert."**

Use Online Reputation Management Services

- **Reputation Management Tools:** Services like DeleteMe, BrandYourself, or Reputation Defender offer options to remove or manage personal information found online.
- **Monitor for Data Broker Listings:** Data brokers often collect and sell public information. Some services can request removal from these lists on your behalf.

When you find **instances of yourself online that you do not agree with**, whether it is misinformation, personal data, or unflattering content, there are several actions you can take depending on the situation and platform:

1. Identify the Source and Type of Content

- Is it on a **social media platform, news site, public records database,** or **forum?**
- Is it **factual but unwanted, inaccurate, harmful,** or **illegal?**

2. Request Removal (Politely and Formally)

- **Contact the site owner or webmaster:**
  - Look for a **"Contact Us"** or **"Report Abuse"** link.
  - Use tools like Whois Lookup to find site contact info. These tools can be found easily online.
- **Use platform-specific reporting tools:**
  - Social media (e.g., Facebook, Twitter, Instagram): Use **"Report"** buttons.
  - Google: Use their **Content Removal Tool** for outdated or sensitive info.

3. Submit a Legal Takedown Request (If Justified)

- **DMCA Takedown:** If the content violates copyright (like a photo you own).
- **Defamation or libel:** You may need legal assistance to send a **cease-and-desist letter** or file a claim.

4. Use Google's "Remove Outdated Content" Tool

- If the content has already been deleted but still shows in search results: https://search.google.com/search-console/remove-outdated-content

5. Suppress It with Positive Content

- Create and promote positive content under your name (blogs, social profiles, LinkedIn, YouTube).
- Google ranks **relevant and recent** content higher; this can push unwanted results down.

6. Consider Professional Help

- **Online reputation management (ORM)** services can help suppress or remove content.
- **Cybersecurity or legal professionals** can assist with more serious

privacy breaches.

Important:

- **Public records** (like court records, property data) are difficult to remove, but you can **request redactions** in some cases.
- Do not engage directly with trolls or hostile posters, this often makes things worse.

Limit Device and App Tracking
Adjust Mobile App Permissions

- **Review App Permissions Regularly:** Disable access to sensitive data for apps that do not need it, like location, contacts, or camera.
- **Turn Off Background Location Tracking:** Only allow location access while using an app to limit the amount of location data shared.

Disable Tracking Features in Devices

- **Limit Device Advertising ID:** Most mobile operating systems offer settings to limit ad tracking. Go to Privacy > Advertising on iOS and Android.
- **Opt Out of Interest-Based Ads:** Disable interest-based ads in your device's settings to reduce data collection for targeted advertising.

Protect Yourself from Data Breaches

- **Sign Up for Alerts:** Some password managers offer breach monitoring and will let you know if your information appears in a data leak.
- Manually opt out of data broker websites (like Whitepages, Spokeo, and MyLife).

Data Removal & Opt-Out Services

You may want to consider services that can help monitor and/or remove your data from danger. These companies help remove your personal information from data broker sites, people search engines, and other online databases. Services like:

- **DeleteMe** (joindeleteme.com) – Offers continuous monitoring and removal of personal data from major data brokers.
- **OneRep** (onerep.com) – Automates the process of opting out of people search sites.
- **Incogni** (incogni.com) – Automates requests for data removal from multiple sources.
- **Privacy Bee** (privacybee.com) – Continuously scans and removes your data from various databases.
- **Optery** (optery.com) – Provides free and paid plans for removing personal information from online sources.

Reputation Management Services

These services help control your online presence by suppressing or removing negative or unwanted content:

- **Reputation Defender** (reputationdefender.com)
- **BrandYourself** (brandyourself.com)
- **NetReputation** (netreputation.com)

Security & Privacy Protection Tools

- **Have I Been Pwned?** (haveibeenpwned.com) – Checks if your email or passwords have been leaked in data breaches.
- **Jumbo Privacy** (jumboprivacy.com) – Helps secure your online accounts, remove old posts, and manage privacy settings.
- **Blur by Abine** (abine.com) – Offers email masking, password management, and identity protection.

Update Compromised Accounts Promptly

- **Change Passwords for Affected Accounts:** When notified of a data breach, update passwords immediately to prevent unauthorized access.
- **Implement Security Best Practices:** Enable 2FA on sensitive accounts and avoid using the same password across multiple platforms to reduce risks.

Conclusion

Managing your digital footprint requires regular monitoring, using privacy tools, and making conscious decisions about the information you share online. By following these practices, adjusting privacy settings, cleaning up old accounts, and minimizing data collection, you can significantly reduce your exposure and maintain greater control over your personal information. Being initiative-taking with privacy helps to ensure a safer, secure digital presence in today's data-driven world.

Chapter 12

Children and Cybersecurity

🔑

Teaching your children to recognize cyberbullying and avoiding communications with strangers online are valuable lessons. You can use parental controls on apps and devices to limit screen time and monitor their online activities as well. Although this may not be one of the top ten priorities for securing your digital life, instilling the appropriate habits into your family now may save them enormous harm in the future.

Children and Cybersecurity at Home: Protecting Young Users Online

As children grow up in an increasingly digital world, they are using the internet to learn, socialize, and play. However, they are also more vulnerable to online threats like inappropriate content, cyberbullying, and identity theft. These activities could also help criminals develop ties with others. By establishing a secure online environment at home, parents can help children develop safe and responsible digital habits. Here is a comprehensive guide to cybersecurity for children in the home.

Educating Children on Cybersecurity Basics
Teach Age-Appropriate Cybersecurity Concepts
- **Passwords and Privacy:** Explain why they should never share their passwords, even with friends. Help them create strong, memorable passwords.
- **The Importance of Privacy:** Discuss the importance of keeping personal information private, such as their full name, address, and school name.
- **Encourage Transparency:** Create an environment where children feel comfortable talking about what they do online and any concerns they have.
- **Set Clear Guidelines:** Establish rules about when and where screens are allowed, what sites can be accessed, and appropriate online behavior.

Cyberbullying Awareness
- Educate them on what cyberbullying is, how to recognize it, and how to respond (e.g., not retaliating, telling a trusted adult).
- **Encourage Empathy and Respect:** Explain the importance of treating others respectfully online and discourage hurtful comments or teasing.
- **Teach How to Report and Block:** Show kids how to report inappropriate behavior and block users who make them uncomfortable.

Develop Critical Thinking About Online Content

- **Identify Phishing and Scams:** Teach children to avoid clicking on suspicious links, especially those that offer "free" gifts or ask for personal information.
- **Misinformation Awareness:** Help kids understand that not everything they see online is true and to question information from unknown sources.

Parental Controls to Create a Safe Online Environment
Parental Controls on Devices

- **On Computers and Mobile Devices:** Most operating systems (Windows, macOS, iOS, Android) offer parental controls to limit access to inappropriate content and apps.
- **Time Restrictions:** Use parental controls to set limits on screen time, helping to balance online and offline activities.

Parental Control Software

- **Software Options:** Tools like **Net Nanny, Bark,** and **Qustodio** offer comprehensive parental controls, including web filtering, app monitoring, and social media tracking.
- **Age-Appropriate Filtering:** Set filters to block adult content, gambling, and violent material. Adjust these filters based on your child's age and maturity level.

Monitor Gaming and Streaming Platforms

- **Set Up Parental Controls on Consoles:** Gaming consoles (Xbox, PlayStation, Nintendo Switch) have parental controls for restricting game content and online interaction.
- **Supervise Streaming Access:** Streaming platforms like YouTube, Netflix, and Disney+ have child-friendly content modes. Set up profiles with age-appropriate restrictions.

Encourage Responsible Social Media Use
Set Age Limits for Social Media Accounts

- **Follow Platform Age Requirements:** Most social media platforms require users to be at least 13 years old. Enforcing these rules helps protect children from mature content and predatory behavior.

- **Discuss the Dangers of Oversharing:** Instruct kids not to post personal information, their real-time location, or photos with identifiable details.

Teach Privacy Settings and Account Security
- **Adjust Privacy Settings Together:** Show children how to make their profiles private and limit who can see their posts.
- **Limit Friends to Real-Life Contacts:** Encourage them to only "friend" people they know in real life, reducing exposure to strangers or potential scammers.

Online Classrooms
- **Use Strong Meeting Passwords:** For Zoom or other virtual classrooms, ensure that sessions are password-protected to prevent unauthorized access.
- **Supervise Classroom Interactions:** Familiarize yourself with online learning tools and occasionally check in to ensure respectful interactions and that your child feels safe.

Ensure Safe Access to Educational Resources
- **Bookmark Trusted Sites:** Create a list of approved, educational websites that children can access for assignments and research.
- **Teach Caution with Unknown Links:** Teach kids to verify unknown links with you or their teacher before clicking on them, as even educational sites can sometimes redirect to ads or malicious content.

Being Aware of Online Friendships
- **Monitor New Friend Requests:** Be aware of who your child is interacting with online, especially if they are meeting new people in games or social apps.
- **Warn About Stranger Danger Online:** Teach children to be cautious when chatting with people they do not know, as predators may pose as peers or friends.

Limit Online Purchases and In-Game Transactions
- **Disable In-App Purchases:** Prevent unapproved purchases by

disabling in-app purchases or adding password protection for transactions.

- **Discuss the Risks of Sharing Financial Information:** Children should understand that they should never share financial information (like card numbers) online.

Model Good Cybersecurity Habits
Be a Role Model in Responsible Internet Use

- **Practice Safe Browsing Habits:** Show children that you avoid suspicious links, use privacy settings, and practice secure internet behavior.
- **Respect Screen-Free Time:** Encourage screen-free time for the whole family to help children develop a balanced approach to technology.

Engage in Online Activities Together

- **Play Online Games Together:** When possible, participate in games or activities that interest your child, allowing you to monitor the content and interactions.
- **Review and Discuss Content:** Help children understand appropriate online content by guiding them through the sites or apps they enjoy and explaining what they should avoid.

Inappropriate Content

- **Use Filters for Content Control:** Implement age-appropriate content filters to block explicit material on search engines, browsers, and streaming services.
- **Encourage Reporting of Inappropriate Content:** Tell children to let you know immediately if they come across something that makes them uncomfortable, reassuring them that they will not get in trouble.

Online Grooming and Predatory Behavior

- **Educate on Safe Interaction Guidelines:** Explain that some people pretend to be someone they are not online and emphasize that they should never meet online friends in real life without a trusted adult present.

Conclusion

Cybersecurity for children at home involves a mix of education, initiative-taking monitoring, and the use of parental controls and privacy settings. By teaching children about online risks and guiding them in safe digital practices, parents can help them develop healthy, responsible online habits. Open communication, clear boundaries, and regular check-ins about online activity allow parents to create a safer digital environment and empower kids to protect their privacy and security online.

HOME AND IoT SECURITY

Chapter 13

Securing Smart Devices in Your Home

🔑

Managing Internet of Things (IoT) devices, such as smart TVs and smart home assistants like Alexa, Google Assistant, or Siri, can be a daunting task. These are technological devices in your home that are often overlooked. Devices like smart cameras (e.g., Ring) and voice assistants (e.g., Alexa) come with important security and privacy considerations.

You do not need to become an expert on these systems, but you should have a general understanding of the risks involved in using them and develop enough skills to maintain them at a reasonable level to protect yourself from potential harm. At a minimum, you should disable purchasing functions to prevent accidental orders and monitor what data your assistant is collecting and sharing with third parties.

Below is a list of the most common IoT devices to help you identify what you may have in your home, so you can review their configurations and secure them better. You will also find general instructions for the most popular devices.

Smart Entertainment
Smart TVs and Streaming Devices
1. **Smart TVs:** Samsung Smart TV, LG OLED, Sony Bravia
2. **Streaming Devices:** Roku, Amazon Fire Stick, Google Chromecast, Apple TV
3. **Smart Sound Systems:** Sonos Speakers, Bose SoundTouch, Yamaha MusicCast

Smart TVs and streaming devices can collect data about your viewing habits and may include invasive advertising settings.

Turn Off Automatic Content Recognition (ACR)
- **Limit Data Collection on Viewing Habits:** ACR technology tracks your viewing patterns to serve personalized ads. Disable it in the settings if privacy is a concern.
- **Review Privacy Settings on Streaming Services:** Each service may have separate privacy settings, so go through each one and adjust as needed to limit data collection.

Restrict Voice Command Features
- **Disable "Always Listening" Modes:** Many smart TVs come with voice command features that continuously listen for prompts. Turn off these features when not in use.
- **Cover Built-in Cameras:** Some smart TVs have built-in cameras. Use a cover if the camera is not needed.

Smart Home Assistants and Hubs
- **Smart Speakers:** Amazon Echo, Google Nest, Apple HomePod
- **Voice-Activated Assistants:** Alexa, Google Assistant, Siri
- **Smart Hubs:** Samsung SmartThings Hub, Hubitat, Wink Hub

Adjust Privacy Settings on Voice Assistants
   o **Delete Recorded Interactions Regularly:** Most voice assistants (like Amazon Alexa, Google Assistant) record interactions. Go into the settings to review and delete these recordings periodically.
   o **Disable or Limit Skills/Integrations:** Some voice assistant skills or integrations may collect additional data. Limit only the essential or trusted one's skills and the ones currently used.

Smart Security Systems
- **Security Cameras:** Nest Cam, Ring, Arlo, Wyze Cam, Blink
- **Video Doorbells:** Ring Doorbell, Nest Hello, Arlo Video Doorbell
- **Smart Locks:** August Smart Lock, Schlage Encode, Yale Assure Lock, Kwikset Halo
- **Alarm Systems:** SimpliSafe, ADT, Ring Alarm, Abode
- **Smart Sensors:** Door/window sensors, motion sensors, glass break sensors
- **Use Security Modes:** Some smart home security systems allow "home" and "away" modes, adjusting access and notifications based on your location. Set these appropriately to avoid unauthorized access. Example: Knowing your away and receiving a notification of a status change will let you know that someone may be in your home.

Smart Lighting
- **Smart Bulbs:** Philips Hue, LIFX, Sengled, TP-Link Kasa
- **Smart Light Switches and Dimmers:** Lutron Caséta, TP-Link, Leviton, Wemo
- **Smart Plugs and Outlets:** Amazon Smart Plug, TP-Link Kasa, Wemo Mini

Smart Climate Control

- **Smart Thermostats:** Nest Thermostat, Ecobee, Honeywell Home, Mysa
- **Smart Fans and Air Purifiers:** Dyson Pure Cool, Xiaomi Smart Air Purifier
- **Smart Radiator Valves:** Tado, Honeywell Evohome

Smart Kitchen Appliances

- **Smart Refrigerators:** Samsung Family Hub, LG Smart InstaView
- **Smart Ovens and Microwaves:** GE Profile Smart Oven, Whirlpool Smart Oven
- **Smart Coffee Makers:** Keurig K-Supreme Plus Smart, Smarter Coffee 2nd Gen
- **Smart Dishwashers:** Bosch Home Connect, LG Smart Dishwasher

Smart Cleaning Devices

- **Robot Vacuums:** iRobot Roomba, Eufy RoboVac, Roborock
- **Robot Mops:** iRobot Braava Jet, ECOVACS Deebot
- **Smart Washing Machines:** LG Smart Washer, Samsung Smart Washer

Smart Health and Fitness Devices

- **Smart Scales:** Withings Body+, Fitbit Aria, Eufy Smart Scale
- Fitness Trackers and Smartwatches: Fitbit, Apple Watch, Garmin
- **Sleep Monitors:** Withings Sleep, Google Nest Hub (sleep tracking features)

Smart Garden and Outdoor Devices

- **Smart Sprinkler Systems:** Rachio, RainMachine, Orbit B-Hyve
- **Smart Outdoor Cameras and Floodlights:** Ring Floodlight Cam, Arlo Pro, Nest Cam Outdoor
- **Smart Grills and Smokers:** Traeger Timberline, Weber iGrill, Green Mountain Grills

Smart Energy Management

- **Smart Power Strips:** TP-Link Kasa, APC Smart Plug

- **Smart Meters and Monitors:** Sense Energy Monitor, Emporia Vue, Neurio
- Solar Panel Management Systems: SolarEdge, Enphase Energy

Smart Appliances for Daily Use
- **Smart Blinds and Curtains:** Somfy, Lutron Serena, Ikea Fyrtur
- **Smart Ceiling Fans:** Haiku Home, Big Ass Fans, Hunter Symphony
- **Smart Toilets and Bidets:** Toto Washlet, Kohler Veil, Brondell Swash

Review your Smart Devices and try to set up Device-Specific Security Features. Many smart devices offer extra layers of security. Enable these options to provide further protection.

Securing your Smartphone

- **Securing Access To Your Smartphone**
  - Set a Strong Passcode
  - Use a PIN, complex password, or biometric features (fingerprint, facial recognition) for unlocking your phone.
  - Configure your phone to lock automatically after a brief period of inactivity.
- **Keep Operating Systems (IOS, Android etc.) Software Up to Date**
  - Install OS Updates Promptly: Regular updates fix security vulnerabilities in the operating system. Activating Automatic Updates will take care of this for you.
  - **Download Apps from Trusted Sources: Only** install apps from official app stores (Google Play Store, Apple App Store).
  - **Update Apps Regularly:** Ensure all apps are up to date, as updates often include security patches. Activate Automatic Updates
  - **Adjust Camera and Microphone Permissions**
  - **Be aware of Cameras When Not in Use:** If you do not need the camera active, you can turn it off or use a physical cover for added privacy.
  - **Restrict Microphone Access:** Some voice assistants can continuously listen for wake words. Adjust settings to limit this or mute the microphone when you are not actively using the device.

- **Enable Anti-Theft Features:**
    - Use built-in tools like "Find My iPhone" or "Find My Device" for remote tracking, locking, or wiping your phone if it is lost or stolen.
- **Perform Test For Potential Harm**
- **Manage Bluetooth and Near Field Communication (NFC)**
    - Turn Off Bluetooth and NFC When Not in Use:
        - This helps prevent unauthorized access via open connections.
        - Only connect to devices you trust.
- **Backup and Encrypt Your Data**
    - Enable Encryption:
        - Use built-in encryption settings to secure your data in case your phone is stolen.
    - Perform Regular Backups:
        - Backup your data to a secure cloud service or external storage.

- **Check For Potential Hacking:** Check to see if anyone has potentially tampered with your phone by using the USSD code (Unstructured Supplementary Service Data) feature to provide quick access to the status of the call forwarding settings on your phone or network.
    - On your mobile phone, Dial *#21# to check the status of call forwarding. If any of these features are activated, you should investigate as to why, if you have not applied these settings yourself. A malicious actor may secretly have activated call forwarding to redirect your calls or messages (e.g., SMS-based OTPs) to their number, enabling them to intercept your calls, password reset codes or sensitive information. A couple of the most dangerous are receiving a code for a password reset to your account. Or cybercriminal performing a SIM Card Swap or SIM Card Hijack where the criminal tricks or bribes a mobile carrier into transferring your phone number over to them!

Limit Cloud Storage and Remote Access

- **Review Cloud Storage Settings:** Many smartphones automatically store footage in the cloud, which may not be encrypted or storing information you do not want to expose. Limit the amount of stored footage and review the privacy policy to understand how data is owned

and managed.
- **Disable External Access to Live Feeds:** Ensure that only trusted users can access your live feeds and stored video. Password-protect and periodically monitor access to prevent unauthorized viewing.

Conclusion

These devices can connect to each other and to centralized home hubs, allowing users to manage and automate their homes with greater convenience and physical security. Securing smart devices in your home is essential to protect your network and personal information. By focusing on network security, keeping devices updated, controlling access, and educating household members, you can create a secure and safe smart home environment. Regular monitoring and adjusting of device settings will help maintain a strong defense against cyber threats, allowing you to enjoy the convenience of smart technology with confidence.

PLANNING FOR THE FUTURE

Chapter 14

Dealing with a Security Breach at Home

Dealing with a Security can be distressing, especially when an attack has occurred and you are in the middle of handling it. When potentially exposing sensitive personal information and compromising devices that will require repair. Whether due to a compromised account, unauthorized access to your network, or malware infection, addressing the breach swiftly and thoroughly is critical to limit damage. Here is a step-by-step guide on how to respond effectively to a security breach at home.

Step 1: Stop the Damage

Remember, this can be time sensitive, harm can be getting performed as time passes.

- **Isolate Affected Devices:** Disconnect compromised devices from the internet to prevent further spread of malware or unauthorized access.
- This includes your Wi-Fi or internet equipment.
  (This allows you to stop any hacker from accessing your technology while you fix things.)

Step 2: Assess, Identify and Isolate all Account Breaches

Regain control of your main online and sensitive accounts: You need a trusted phone or computer you believe to be unharmed to perform the next steps. If you are not sure your PC has not been corrupted, disconnect it from the internet and run an Antivirus/Malware tool to validate, clean, and establish a trusted system before proceeding to the next step. You can always call the institutions directly to lock your accounts down or have them reset a temporary password.

Change your passwords immediately.

- Begin with your main email account (Gmail, Outlook, iCloud/Apple, and Password Manger accounts). You want to target the accounts you use for identity validation, Multi-Factor Authentication, and password management.
- Login and change your password to a new, strong one.
- Turning on 2-Step Verification now if you have not already could help prevent this from recurring. *(They will text or call you to confirm it is you.)*
- Check for:
  - "Recent activity"
  - "Devices signed in"
  - "Security alerts"
  - Remove anyone or anything listed on the account like trusted systems (systems you log in from) that is not yours.
  - Remove any "forwarding rules" you did not set up
  - Delete any filters that hide or reroute mail
  (If you are calling into your service organizations because you do not have access to a

trusted system, they can help perform some of these tasks for you.)
Secure any linked accounts:
- Banking apps, Amazon, social media, etc that link to one another. *(These often get hijacked after email.)*

Notify banks or other services if you believe sensitive financial data might have been compromised.

Inform your workplace IT team if you believe your workplace computer has been compromised.

Step 3: Determine the Scope of all Breaches
After you have recovered and secured your main accounts and sensitive information, try to identify obvious affected devices and less-sensitive accounts.
- **Check for unusual behavior on devices** (like slow performance, unexpected pop-ups) and review account activity logs for unfamiliar logins.
- **Look for Signs of Compromise:** Common signs include receiving password reset notifications, unusual account transactions, and changes in security settings.

Step 4: Clean Your Computer (If Needed)
If anything, strange happened on your device (like pop-ups, slowness, or unknown apps):
1. Restart your PC in Safe Mode to prevent malware from running and spreading further. To do this:
   - Restart your PC.
   - When the Startup Settings screen appears, Press your 5 key or F5 at the list to enter Safe Mode with Networking.
   - **Run Antivirus and malware Scans:** Hopefully, you have acquired Antivirus software by now. If not, I would recommend acquiring one at this point and running antivirus and malware scans on all systems. In a pinch, you can download basic versions for free like (e.g., Malwarebytes, Norton, or Kaspersky-Free Versions). While

they may offer premium upgrades, their free versions are effective for basic threat detection and removal:

- o **Microsoft Defender (Built into Windows 10/11)**
  - **Type**: Antivirus & malware protection
  - **Strengths**: Real-time protection, regular updates
  - *Highly recommended for Windows users*
- o **Malwarebytes Free**
  - **Type**: Anti-malware
  - **Strengths**: Excellent at finding threats traditional antivirus may miss
  - **Note**: Free version does not offer real-time protection, manual scans only
- o **Bitdefender Antivirus Free Edition**
  - **Type**: Antivirus
  - **Strengths**: Lightweight, minimal setup, strong protection
- o **Avast Free Antivirus**
  - **Type**: Antivirus & malware
  - **Strengths**: Easy interface, decent protection
  - **Note**: Watch for optional installations during setup
- o **Kaspersky Security Cloud – Free**
  - **Type**: Antivirus
  - **Strengths**: Strong detection rates
  - **Note**: Tends to be affective, but it is based in Russia, some users avoid it for geopolitical concerns

Update Your Operating System and Software

Install the latest updates to patch vulnerabilities.

Restore from Backup (if necessary)

If possible, restore your system to a state before the suspected hack. Use a backup you know is clean.

Reset Your PC (if necessary)

If the issue persists, consider performing a factory reset or clean installation of your operating system and restore from backups.

Step 5: Strengthen Everything

- **Turn on MFA (2-step login) for all accounts — not just email.**

- Use a password manager (like Bitwarden, 1Password, or Apple Keychain).
- Never reuse passwords between accounts.
- Update your device software and apps.
- Change your Wi-Fi router password (especially if you never have before).

Additional Free applications that may help clean a compromised PC.
🌑 🌑 🌑 *Disclaimer: A couple of the later tools in this list are serious tools, but if you are at the point of needing a system rebuild, what is the harm, correct! Start with the first couple and if they do not help, you have a severe problem.*

1. Hitman Pro
2. RKill
3. RogueKiller
4. Tron 🌑 🌑 🌑

When to Seek Professional Help
You may need to consider consulting a cybersecurity professional for a thorough review if the breach is overwhelming, or you are experiencing the issues below to reduce further damage or spread.

- **Persistent Issues:** If malware removal tools cannot resolve the issue.
- **Data Breach:** If sensitive personal or financial information is exposed.
- **System Compromise:** If you suspect advanced threats like rootkits or ransomware.

Step 6: Secure Your Home Network (if necessary)
Reboot and Reset Your Internet Router
- **Update Your Router's Firmware:** Check your router's firmware for updates to ensure you have the latest security patches.

Change Wi-Fi Network Name and Password
- **Create a New, Strong Wi-Fi Password:** Choose a complex password that is different from the previous one and avoid using identifiable information in the network name (SSID). Note: Passwords must be updated on connected devices to regain access.

- **Use WPA3 Encryption if Available:** WPA3 is the most secure Wi-Fi encryption standard. If your router does not support WPA3, use WPA2 as the next best option.

Create a Separate Network for IoT and Guest Devices
- **Isolate IoT Devices on a Separate Network:** If your router supports it, setting up a separate network for smart devices will help limit their access to your main network, reducing potential entry points for hackers.

Step 7: Inform Financial Institutions and Monitor Accounts (if you have been compromised)

Notify Your Bank and Credit Card Companies
- **Report Suspicious Transactions Immediately:** If your financial information was compromised, inform your bank or credit card provider so they can freeze accounts or issue new cards.
- **Consider Freezing Your Credit:** In cases of identity theft, a credit freeze can prevent new accounts from being opened in your name.
- **Check Credit Monitoring Services:** If you have acquired Credit Monitoring Services through one of the credit monitoring companies directly or your antivirus solution, check for invalid charges or suspicious activity.

Monitor Financial Accounts Closely
- **Enable Alerts for Transactions:** Most banks offer email or SMS alerts for transactions, helping you catch unauthorized purchases quickly.
- **Check Credit Reports Regularly:** Why check your credit report? Your report shows things like how many credit cards and loans you have, whether you pay your bills on time, and whether any debts have been turned over to collections. Creditors, insurers, some employers, and other businesses use it to decide if they want to do business with you, and the terms they will offer you. Use can use free credit report services like AnnualCreditReport.com to check for any unfamiliar accounts or inquiries. As of 2023, the three national credit reporting agencies, Equifax, Experian, and TransUnion, have permanently extended a program that lets you check your credit report at each of the agencies

once a week for free.

Step 8: Re-Establish Security on IoT Devices (if necessary)

Reset IoT Devices to Factory Settings
- **Wipe Compromised Devices:** If your smart devices were compromised, reset them to factory settings to remove unauthorized access and any potential malware.
- **Update Firmware and Software:** Check for firmware updates for IoT devices to ensure they are running the latest security patches.

Use Strong, Unique Passwords for Each Device
- **Avoid Default Passwords:** Always change the default passwords on smart devices, as these are often publicly available and easy for hackers to guess.
- **Enable Two-Factor Authentication:** If your IoT device app offers 2FA, enable it to add an extra layer of protection.

Step 9: Strengthening Security Practices Going Forward
Create a Routine for Regular Updates
- **Enable Automatic Updates for Devices and Software:** Automatic updates ensure that your devices stay protected against the latest threats.
- **Update Router Firmware Regularly:** Check for router firmware updates every few months, as routers often do not update automatically.

Step 10: Educating Household Members on Cybersecurity Practices
- **Share Security Guidelines with Family Members:** Inform everyone in your home about the importance of strong passwords, identifying phishing emails, and safe internet use.
- **Encourage Caution with Emails and Links:** Teach family members to be wary of unsolicited links or attachments, as these are common sources of malware.

Step 11: Conduct a Security Audit of Your Home Network
Review of All Devices Connected to Your Network ◖

- **Create a List of All Connected Devices:** Inventory every device connected to your network (computers, phones, tablets, smart TVs, IoT devices).
- **Check Each Device's Security Settings:** Make sure all devices have updated security settings, including strong passwords, current firmware, and enabled firewalls.

Step 12: Perform a Penetration Test on Your Network ◖

- **Run a Self-Assessment Test:** Advanced users can use tools like Nmap or Nessus to evaluate vulnerabilities on their home network.
- **Consider Professional Help:** If you are not comfortable conducting penetration tests, consult a cybersecurity professional for a security assessment.

Step 13: Reporting Breaches and Learning from Incidents
Report Identity Theft or Fraud to Authorities

- **File a Report with Your Local Authorities:** In cases of financial fraud or identity theft, it may help to file a report with your local police department. However, if you are aware of a new widespread attack, or an event involving large sums of money, you should notify the FBI's Internet Crime Complaint Center (IC3) as this may give them an early indicator of an act of terrorism. Also, if you notify them early enough, they can sometimes prevent a loss of funds.
- **Report to Cybersecurity Organizations:** Contact organizations like the Federal Trade Commission (FTC) or IdentityTheft.gov for guidance on handling identity theft.

Step 14: Learn from the Incident to Prevent Future Breaches

- **Analyze How the Breach Occurred:** Review what might have led to the breach, such as weak passwords, phishing, or unpatched software.
- **Adopt Stronger Security Measures:** Use the lessons learned to implement stronger security protocols at home, like regularly updating devices and improving password hygiene.

Conclusion

Dealing with a security breach at home requires immediate action to identify the compromised devices and accounts, secure access, and prevent further unauthorized activity. By following these steps, isolating the breach, updating passwords, securing your network, and monitoring accounts, you can regain control over your home's cybersecurity. Developing a proactive security routine and educating household members can also help prevent future incidents, ensuring a safer and more secure home environment.

Chapter 15

Staying Informed About New Cyber Threats

🔑

Follow trusted cybersecurity sources and participate in webinars or courses to stay updated on emerging threats.

Staying Informed About New Cyber Threats at Home

Cyber threats are constantly evolving, with new malware, phishing scams, and vulnerabilities emerging regularly. Staying informed about these threats can help maintain a secure home environment, protecting personal data, and ensuring your devices remain safe from the latest tactics used by cybercriminals. Choose some and stay informed as though you would top news topics today. Here is a guide to staying updated on cybersecurity threats and adopting practices that enhance your home security.

Follow Reputable Cybersecurity News Sources
Subscribe to Cybersecurity News Websites
- **Popular News Outlets:** Websites like **Krebs on Security, Threatpost,** and **The Hacker News** provide daily updates on cybersecurity issues, including emerging threats, vulnerabilities, and best practices.
- **Government Resources:** Websites like US-CERT (Cybersecurity & Infrastructure Security Agency) or StaySafeOnline (National Cyber Security Alliance) offer regular advisories on current cyber threats, especially those affecting general consumers.

Sign Up for Threat Alerts and Newsletters
Use Government Alerts and Bulletins
- **CISA Alerts:** The Cybersecurity & Infrastructure Security Agency (CISA), a department under the Department of Defense (DoD) provides alerts on major cyber incidents and vulnerabilities, offering practical advice for securing systems. They provide various levels of these alerts from individuals and families to technology professionals. These updates are typically released timely and many times before mainstream media releases them. Here is how to sign up for these alerts:

1. **Go to the official CISA subscription page:** https://www.cisa.gov/subscribe
2. **Enter your email address** in the subscription box and click **"Submit."**
3. On the next screen, **check the box next to:**
   - **National Cyber Awareness System** (This includes Alerts, Tips, Vulnerability Bulletins, and Current Activity)
4. (Optional) You can also check:
   - Cybersecurity Advisories
   - CISA Tips and Resource Updates
5. Click **"Submit"** again to confirm your choices.
6. **Check your email** and click the confirmation link to activate your

subscription.

What You'll Receive:

- **Easy-to-understand cybersecurity alerts.**
- **Weekly summaries** of new threats and recommended actions
- **Tips** tailored for individuals, families, and small businesses.

Subscribe to Cybersecurity Newsletters

- **Weekly and Monthly Updates:** Many cybersecurity sites offer newsletters that summarize major security news. **BleepingComputer, Dark Reading**, and **Wired Security** offer quality summaries of top threats and guidance on protecting against them.
- **Home Security Focus:** Some newsletters, like Norton's **Cyber Safety Pulse**, focus on threats specific to personal and home use, offering practical tips for users of all experience levels.

Set Up Google Alerts for Cybersecurity Topics

- **Track Specific Topics:** Google Alerts allows you to receive notifications on cybersecurity terms like "phishing," "ransomware," or "data breach." Customize your alerts to get updates on threats that may impact your devices or home setup. Here is how:
    1. **Go to** https://www.google.com/alerts
    2. In the **search box at the top**, type a cybersecurity topic you want to monitor. Examples:
        - cybersecurity threats
        - ransomware attacks
        - data breaches
        - zero-day vulnerability
        - phishing scams
        - "home network" AND cybersecurity
    3. Click the **"Show options"** link to customize:
        - **How often**: Choose how often you want alerts (e.g., once a day, as it happens)
        - **Sources**: News, blogs, web, etc. (you can leave this as "Automatic")
        - **Language**: English (or your preferred language)

- **Region**: Any or your country
- **How many**: Only the best results, or all results
- **Deliver to**: Choose your email address.

4. Click **"Create Alert."**
5. Repeat for other topics or keywords you want to track.

Tips for Better Alerts:
Use **quotation marks** to search for exact phrases like: "cybersecurity for seniors."
Use **AND / OR** to combine keywords: "smart home" AND security.

Follow Cybersecurity Experts on Social Media

- **X (Twitter), LinkedIn, and Reddit:** Follow cybersecurity experts and organizations on social platforms where they often share insights, breaking news, and quick advice on handling recent threats.
- **Popular Accounts to Follow:** Consider experts like Brian Krebs (@briankrebs), Graham Cluley (@gcluley), and cybersecurity organizations like **EFF (Electronic Frontier Foundation)** and **SANS Institute**.

Leverage Cybersecurity Tools with Threat Detection Features

Use Antivirus and Antimalware with Real-Time Protection

- **Enable Threat Notifications:** Many antivirus programs (like Norton, Bitdefender, or Kaspersky) offer threat notifications when new malware or vulnerabilities are detected. Keep real-time protection enabled to receive these alerts.
- **Check for Threat Intelligence Updates:** Many premium antivirus and security software offer "threat intelligence" or "threat insight" features that provide alerts on new risks.

Set Up Network Monitoring for Suspicious Activity

- **Use Network Monitoring Tools:** Tools like **Fing** or **GlassWire** help monitor your network for unknown devices, unusual traffic, and unauthorized access attempts, keeping you aware of potential threats in real-time.

- **Regularly Review Router Security Logs:** Many modern routers provide logs of incoming and outgoing connections. Review these logs periodically to identify any unauthorized access attempts.

Participate in Cybersecurity Awareness Training and Resources

There are many free or low-cost cybersecurity training offerings. Here are some of the best free cybersecurity training resources available, especially for home users, students, and small business owners looking to improve their knowledge and protect themselves:

1. **CISA – Cybersecurity Awareness Training**
   - Link: https://www.cisa.gov
   - Topics: Basic cyber hygiene, phishing, social engineering, securing devices
   - Why it is great: Government-backed, beginner-friendly, and includes printable materials and tips.

2. **StaySafeOnline (NCA)**
   - Link: https://staysafeonline.org
   - Run by: National Cybersecurity Alliance
   - Topics: Password safety, Wi-Fi security, mobile protection, online shopping safety
   - Why it is great: Engaging, non-technical, and tailored for individuals and families.

3. **Cybrary**
   - Link: https://www.cybrary.it
   - Topics: Cybersecurity fundamentals, network security, threat intelligence
   - Why it is great: Offers beginner to intermediate technical training;

some free courses and career paths.

4. **IBM SkillsBuild Cybersecurity Basics**
   - Link: https://skillsbuild.org
   - Topics: Cyber threats, safety fundamentals, career readiness
   - Why it is great: Includes video lessons, quizzes, and badges, great for both learning and resumes.

5. **Open Security Training**
   - Link: http://opensecuritytraining.info
   - Topics: Technical cybersecurity (more advanced topics like reverse engineering and malware analysis)
   - Why it is great: Free for those who want to go deeper into security concepts.

6. **YouTube Channels (Trusted Sources)**
   - Examples:
   - NetworkChuck – fun, hands-on training
   - David Bombal – network security, ethical hacking basics
   - CISA's own YouTube channel – practical safety tips and national updates

7. **Google's Be Internet Awesome (for Families)**
   - Link: https://beinternetawesome.withgoogle.com
   - Why it is great: Teaches kids and families how to spot scams, create strong passwords, and stay safe online in a game-like format.
   - Cybersecurity Webinars: Attend webinars by organizations like CISA, Norton, or AVG that provide insights on protecting against current threats, especially those targeting individuals and home networks.

Use Family-Focused Cybersecurity Resources

- **StaySafeOnline:** This site offers family-friendly resources on common threats, helping all household members learn about cybersecurity in an approachable way.
- **Interactive Cyber Safety Games for Kids:** Websites like CyberSafe

and NetSmartz provide educational games for children, teaching them about online safety while making it fun.

Learn from Recent Cybersecurity Incidents
Track High-Profile Data Breaches
- **Breach Reports and Security Bulletins:** Whenever there is a large-scale data breach (such as Equifax or Facebook), review news and reports to understand what led to the breach and the lessons learned for improving security.

Research New Phishing and Scamming Techniques
- **Stay Informed on Phishing Trends:** Phishing tactics evolve constantly. Watch for updates on the latest phishing scams and ensure your household knows how to recognize them.
- **Participate in Phishing Simulations:** Some security companies offer phishing simulations for home users, which simulate phishing attempts to help you learn to recognize and avoid them.

Enable Notifications and Updates on Key Devices 🛡
Keep Software, Firmware, and OS Updated
- **Enable Automatic Updates:** Automatic updates ensure that your devices receive security patches promptly, which are often released in response to emerging threats.
- **Update IoT Device Firmware:** IoT devices often get firmware updates that fix vulnerabilities. Check for updates regularly and apply them as soon as they are available.

Set Up Security Alerts on Devices 🛡
- **Enable Security Notifications:** Many smart home devices and apps offer security alerts for login attempts, access from new devices, or firmware updates. Enable these alerts to stay informed of activity.
- **Use Router Security Features:** Routers like those from Netgear and

ASUS often have built-in alerts for suspicious activity. Enable these notifications in your router settings.

Conclusion

Staying informed about new cyber threats at home involves a mix of proactive learning, using technology to monitor and secure devices, and adopting strong digital habits. By keeping up with cybersecurity news, attending online training, and leveraging tools with built-in threat detection, you can stay one step ahead of emerging threats. Engaging household members in cybersecurity practices and maintaining a routine of regular updates and security checks will create a safer and more resilient home network.

Chapter 16

The Personal Cybersecurity Checklist

This personal cybersecurity checklist contains the key information most home users need. It outlines the top ten priority tasks that will help you maintain a secure digital environment at home by covering essential security steps and best practices, including how to educate household members on safe online habits.

---

1. **Use Strong, Unique Passwords**
   What to do: Create passwords that are long and complex, and unique for each account.

Why it matters: Weak or reused passwords are one of the most common ways hackers break in.

2. **Turn On Multi-Factor Authentication (MFA)**
   What to do: Enable MFA wherever possible (email, banking, cloud storage, etc.), using an authenticator app or hardware token.
   Why it matters: Even if a hacker steals your password, MFA adds an extra barrier to keep your accounts safe.

3. **Keep Devices and Software Updated**
   What to do: Enable automatic updates for your operating system, browsers, apps, and smart devices.
   Why it matters: Updates patch security holes that attackers could exploit.

4. **Secure Your Home Wi-Fi Network**
   What to do: Change the default router name and password, use WPA3 or WPA2 encryption, and disable remote management.
   Why it matters: Your Wi-Fi is the gateway to your home network, do not let it be an open door.

5. **Use Antivirus and Anti-Malware Tools**
   What to do: Install and regularly scan with reputable security software like Microsoft Defender or Malwarebytes.
   Why it matters: These tools can detect and remove threats before they cause damage.

6. **Back Up Your Important Data**
   What to do: Use the 3-2-1 backup rule: 3 copies of your files, 2 types of storage (e.g., cloud + USB), 1 off-site.
   Why it matters: Ransomware, hardware failure, or accidents can wipe out irreplaceable data.

7. **Watch for Phishing and Scams**
   What to do: Do not click on suspicious links or attachments. Verify unexpected requests through a known, separate channel.
   Why it matters: Phishing emails and texts are a leading cause of identity

theft and account takeovers.

8. **Limit What You Share Online**
   What to do: Review your social media privacy settings and avoid posting personal info like your birthday, address, or vacation plans.
   Why it matters: Cybercriminals gather personal data to answer security questions or impersonate you.

9. **Monitor Accounts and Devices**
   What to do: Set up login alerts, review account activity regularly, and use tools like HaveIBeenPwned to check for breaches.
   If you have not already acquired monitoring services, I would highly recommend it. Some antivirus solutions have these features built-in. If yours does not, you can go directly to your credit services or utilize other tools as mentioned in this book to monitor your credit, your online accounts, your mortgage, and car titles, and much more. This service will go a long way in protecting your digital life, and I believe it will become common place for indiviguals in the future.
   Why it matters: Catching suspicious activity early helps you stop identity theft before it escalates.

10. **Secure Smart Home Devices (IoT)**
    What to do: Change default usernames/passwords, keep firmware updated, and consider isolating these devices on a guest network.
    Why it matters: Smart devices like cameras, thermostats, and doorbells can be vulnerable entry points.

Final Tips
- **Stay Informed About New Cyber Threats:** Follow reputable cybersecurity sites (like CISA, Threatpost, or Krebs on Security) to stay updated on the latest threats and security advice.
- **Enable Notifications for Account Changes:** Most major accounts offer notifications for login attempts, password changes, or other significant actions.
- **Use Parental Controls If You Have Children at Home:** Set up parental controls on devices and internet access to protect young users

from inappropriate content and online risks.

Conclusion

By following this cybersecurity checklist, you create a solid foundation for protecting your home's digital environment, securing your devices, and minimizing risks to personal data and accounts. Regularly updating and reviewing this checklist will help you adapt to new threats and maintain a safer, more secure digital home.

Chapter 17

Final Thoughts

Cybersecurity is a continuous effort. The digital landscape evolves, with new threats emerging every day. It is crucial to stay proactive rather than reactive. Just as we lock our doors at night, we need to adopt habits that protect our digital lives. Home cybersecurity requires consistent effort, vigilance, and initiative-taking practices to keep your digital life safe. By implementing layered security, staying informed about the latest threats, and cultivating cybersecurity awareness among household members, you can create a resilient defense against cyber risks. Adopting a routine of regular security checks, strong passwords, and data backups ensures that you are prepared for potential issues while maintaining a safe and secure digital environment at home. Following these best practices strengthens your defenses and provides peace of mind in a connected world.

Acknowledgements

This book would not have been possible without the support and guidance of many individuals.

To my extended family, daughters-in-law, and friends, thank you for always being there with a listening ear and valuable advice. Your understanding and encouragement have meant the world to me.

I would like to extend my deepest gratitude to William Metcalf, a former colleague and a valued friend, whose unwavering dedication to the field of cybersecurity has not only helped shape its evolution but has also profoundly influenced my own professional journey and the creation of this book. Will is a Distinguished Engineer, a respected leader in Cybersecurity Threat Detection, and the co-founder of leading security research and rule-based detection companies. His contributions continue to elevate the field and inspire those who work alongside him.

I also wish to express special thanks to Paul Schmiege and David "Dave" Snell, two highly respected subject-matter experts, for their technical insight and guidance in helping ensure the accuracy and quality of this work.

Paul Schmiege, CISSP, CISA, MISM, currently leads the Security Risk Management team at a major Midwest electric utility. With deep expertise in utility-sector cybersecurity, Paul oversees key areas such as Security Awareness, Cybersecurity Policy, Third-Party Risk Management, NERC CIP Information Compliance, Business Continuity, Insider Threat Programs, and Cybersecurity Assessments. Previously, he was instrumental in launching and leading the utility's first Security Operations Center (SOC), where he implemented advanced toolsets, robust operational processes, and comprehensive staff training.
Paul actively contributes to the cybersecurity community as a member of the Southwest Power Pool's Security Advisory Group (SECAG) and is a recognized speaker on SOC charter development and operational best practices. His work plays a critical role in protecting regional energy infrastructure against evolving cyber threats.

David "Dave" Snell, Senior Network Engineer and Technology Specialist for the City of Kansas City, Missouri, is a veteran technologist with over 30 years of experience securing complex technology environments. As the lead architect for the city's data centers and digital infrastructure, Dave designed and implemented some of the most extensive and diverse municipal technology operations in the region. His deep understanding of operational resiliency, digital transformation, and infrastructure security brings invaluable perspective to this book. Dave's contributions offer readers a real-world view into securing digital systems at the civic scale.

My sincere thanks to Roger and Joyce Strassburg for their tireless editing and thoughtful commentary on each chapter. Your attention to detail and clear guidance were invaluable.

To my employees and coworkers, your unwavering support, and tireless collaboration have been invaluable. Thank you for enduring long hours and standing by me during the most demanding times.

To my mentors, and the management team at the City of Kansas City, Missouri, thank you for nurturing my curiosity and encouraging me to push boundaries. A special acknowledgment to the mayors, city managers, and city council members I had the honor to work with over the years. Your confidence in my abilities inspired me to lead one of the most technologically innovative, and best-protected cities in the world.

To the contributors, advisers, and sources of information, this book stands on the foundation of your knowledge and expertise. Your conversations, research, and insights have deeply enriched this work. I am grateful for your time and generosity.

I am profoundly grateful to each of you. This book is, in so many ways, a reflection of your impact on my life. Thank you for being part of this journey.

Permissions and Source Credits

This book includes material referenced, adapted, or reprinted with permission from several trusted organizations and sources. Every effort has been made to credit original contributors and comply with licensing or usage terms. The following sources are gratefully acknowledged:

- Some content and information in this publication have been sourced from publicly available materials provided by the United States federal government, including but not limited to the **Federal Bureau of Investigation (FBI), Cybersecurity and Infrastructure Security Agency (CISA), Department of Defense (DoD)**, and other affiliated agencies. These sources are used in accordance with applicable public domain usage rights. The author does not claim ownership of such government-produced materials, and their inclusion does not imply endorsement by any federal agency.
- **Ian Barker**. (2022). How long would it take to crack your password?. betanews.com. Retrieved from: https://betanews.com/2023/05/17/how-long-would-it-take-to-crack-your-password/
- **Corey Neskey** (2025), Are Your Passwords in the Green?, www.hivesystems.com
- https://www.hivesystems.com/blog/are-your-passwords-in-the-green?utm_source=tabletext
- Krebs, Brian. "The Target Breach, By the Numbers." Krebs on Security, May 6, 2014, https://krebsonsecurity.com/2014/05/the-target-breach-by-the-numbers/.
- This book incorporates material from Wikipedia, which is available under the **Creative Commons Attribution-ShareAlike License (CC BY-SA 4.0) International License**. Wikipedia® is a registered trademark of the Wikimedia Foundation, Inc., a non-profit organization. All such content has been adapted in accordance with the license's terms, and proper attribution has been made where applicable and in accordance with the license requirements:

Where applicable, modifications and adaptations have been made to suit the context and formatting of this book. A full list of Wikipedia articles used, along with original URLs and revision dates, is available upon request.

Screenshots or product references are the property of their respective trademark owners and are used here for educational and comparative purposes.

Disclaimer and Acknowledgements

About the Author

With over 40 years of experience in the field of technology, David has witnessed the remarkable transformation of the digital landscape, from its earliest stages to today's cutting-edge advancements. His journey began in the mid-1970s, a time when making a mobile telephone call required verbal instructions to an operator. He vividly recalls the moment a major telecommunications company approached him with the opportunity to pioneer the bleeding edge technology of internet services, then known as the "Super Information Highway", to his organization. At that time, dial-up connections were still scarce, and dedicated internet services (and email) were groundbreaking. Yet David foresaw the profound impact this technology would have, a vision that proved invaluable to his organization and the world at large. It was just one of many rewarding decisions that defined his career.

Among his proudest achievements was leading one of the first cities in the world to acquire Google Fiber, setting a new benchmark for internet service. In 2010, when David championed Google Fiber and gigabit connectivity in Kansas City, skeptics doubted its feasibility, and major internet providers deemed it impossible. Today, that endeavor has become one of Kansas City's most valuable assets, with gigabit internet now a goal for most communities.

Throughout his career, David has been privileged to lead Kansas City, Missouri, as one of the largest and most innovative technology hubs on the global stage. His expertise and vision were frequently sought by cities and media worldwide, and he collaborated extensively with organizations including the Center for Internet Security (CIS), the Cybersecurity and Infrastructure Security Agency (CISA), the Department of Homeland Security (DHS), the Federal Bureau of Investigation (FBI), and the White House Administration, on critical cybersecurity and technology matters. His leadership earned him a National Technology Innovation of the Year Award and an unblemished record in cybersecurity throughout his tenure.

Key Achievements

- Retired Chief Information Officer – City of Kansas City, Missouri

- Technology Lead for one of the pioneering and most successful Smart Cities

- Advisory Board Member for Digital Government

- Advisory Board Member for the Mid-America Regional Council Cybersecurity Task Force

- Technology Lead for the pioneering city of Google Fiber

- Managed the Mid-America Regional Surveillance System, encompassing over 7,000 cameras, supporting the Kansas City Chiefs, Kansas City Royals, regional governments, and the Coast Guard's Missouri River Patrol

- Technology Lead for Kansas City during the Major League Baseball 2012 All-Star Game and festivities

- Technology Lead for Kansas City during the Kansas City Chiefs playoff games and championship parades

- Technology Lead for Kansas City during the Kansas City Royals playoff games and World Series parade

David's accomplishments reflect not only his technical expertise but also the dedication and innovation of his teams, who consistently pushed the boundaries of what is possible in technology. From building innovative solutions to orchestrating seamless digital experiences for high-profile events, his career has been both extraordinary and deeply fulfilling.

Help protect everyone by doing your part to stay:

CYBER SAFE